# WAR AND POLITICS

# WAR AND POLITICS

## Understanding Revolutionary Warfare

Gautam Navlakha

Setu Prakashani

Kolkata Delhi

War and Politics : Understanding Revolutionary Warfare
*by* Gautam Navlakha

First Edition : January, 2014
Cover Design : Saema Hussain

ISBN: 978-93-80677-54-5



*Published by:*
Archana Das & Subrata Das
on behalf of **Setu Prakashani**
12/A Sankar Ghosh Lane, Kolkata - 700 006
Phone : +91 33 2219 0704, +91 94330 74548
*e*-mail : setuprakashani@gmail.com
Website : www.setuprakashani.com

*Kolkata Outlet:*
2, Shyama Charan Dey Street,
Kolkata - 700 073

*Delhi Outlet:*
A5, Christian Colony, Patel Chest
(Near Delhi University North Campus)
Delhi - 110 007

Price : Rupees Two Hundred Twenty Five

*Setting by:*
Cynosure, 26, Jodhpur Garden, Kolkata - 700 045
*Printed by:*
Imprinta, 143/2B, A.P.C. Road, Kolkata - 700 006

*To those who died fighting*
*for the emancipation of*
*Indian people from the*
*curse of oppression and exploitation*

# Contents

# Preface

This book is an attempt to understand the specificity and significance of war, in particular, revolutionary warfare. I attempt to do so by analysing revolutionary warfare which the Communist Party of India (Maoist) describes as the Protracted People's War (PPW). Much as I would have liked to analyse the evolution of their military capability, especially war strategy and field tactics, lack of authentic documentation prevents me from attempting this. Instead, I have a modest ambition to seek to dispel some commonly held misconceptions about the place of war in social life as well as to distinguish revolutionary warfare from other forms of warfare.

Indian scholarship on war and peace is patchy. Absence of violence is equated with peace, but the definition of violence grossly underplays structural violence. So peace in an internal war situation is nothing more than restoring the status quo ante. Also, in India much attention is focused on the repeal or amendment of the Armed Forces Special Powers Act (AFSPA) as though the impunity enjoyed by the armed forces rests on AFSPA alone. It is little realized that this impunity is derived through institutional bias in favour of the armed forces, by way of legal entitlements and exceptions, presumption of 'good faith' and 'active duty' that is supposed to go on for twenty-four hours. In other words, any 'act' committed during 'active duty' falls within the purview of the security forces' own court and is further protected by the presumption of 'good faith'. But there is *no* movement in India against the government's propensity to prosecute wars against its own people. (See Annexure.)

Besides, anyone troubled by the deep social cleavage, the relentless struggle by the poor to survive, the recurrent nightmare of depending on an officious and arrogant administration, with the corrupt and the powerful ruling the roost . . . cannot but wish for a social change which lifts the majority of India's billion people out of their degrading existence, to become makers of their own destiny and become the sovereign, as they are supposed to be. To continue to believe that this predatory State can still be made to work for the benefit of the people may be the opinion of some. But there are many who believe that this system is incapable of delivering without an overhaul because it is loaded in favour of the rich, privileged and powerful who do not hesitate to take recourse to tyranny to maintain this system. Yes, individuals do at times get justice. People's pressure does push political parties to enact welfare legislations. Elections do throw out a corrupt or repressive party from the government. But this does not end the cycle of oppression or exploitation. From the making of law to its implementation and from fighting to prevent its subversion to enabling and empowering people, the processes show how well-entrenched the oppressors are. It is remarkable that a scam-ridden ruling party can still push through policies which benefit foreign and domestic capital, offering them incentives and massive subsidies without much ado. The Union Finance Minister in his budget speech on 28 February 2013 made abundantly clear what the government's priority was. According to him, 'India does not have the choice between welcoming and spurning foreign investment. If I may be frank, foreign investment is an imperative.' So it becomes of utmost importance to open up India to foreign investment and succumb to their pressure to cut government spending in social sector and provide security, legal and military, for their investments in areas considered 'risky'. India's corporate sector not only pays a lower corporate tax than their brethrens elsewhere (at 32.5 per cent, it is lower than 40 per cent in the USA, 38 per cent in Japan) but also get subsidies in the form of tax waivers of Rs 5,73,000 crore (the figure for 2012–13), nearly thrice the subsidy for other sectors, which was worth Rs 2,20,000 crore for the same period. As the Receipt Budget for 2013–14 points out, the corporate sector also pays an effective tax rate 10 per cent lower than the tax demanded. So the 'fat cats' continue to prosper and project their demand as what the 'nation' needs because they control the corporate electronic and print media, with the who's who of India's corporate world as owner/investor. In this sense, it is good that the CPI (Maoists) refuse to give up their goal of seizing power, which keeps the fire of rebellion smouldering, because they defy the conventional wisdom which propagates that there is no 'alternative' to the present order of things; this 'wisdom' pushes people into believing that they have no option but to accept the status quo or at best tinker with it to provide some relief for some sections of people.

For Indian military-strategic thinking, *perhaps* it is Colonel E.C. Callwell who is important. The reason being that just as the British Indian Army fought wars of suppression of Indian people, the Indian Army following the transfer of power did the same. Callwell explains in his classic *Small Wars* that

> campaigns for the subjugation of insurrections, for repression of lawlessness, or for the pacification of territories conquered or annexed stand on very

> different footing. They are necessarily internal not external campaigns.

And then goes on to say that

> [t]he crushing of a populace in arms and the stamping out of widespread disaffection by military methods is a harassing form of warfare even in a civilized country with a settled social system; in remote region peopled by half-civilised races or wholly savage tribes such campaigns are most difficult to bring to a satisfactory conclusion, and are always most trying to the troops.[1]

Such thinking is not alien to the Indian government and its military even if the reason for waging such wars comes wrapped in packages such as 'for development', or 'to protect India's secular democracy', or 'to protect its territorial integrity'.

Those who eulogize peaceful movements believe that the existing institutions could be made more responsive to people's needs. But what they fail to address is the question that when people, or a section of people, feel that their survival is at stake and it's a matter of self-preservation, do they have any other choice than to fight back physically? It is also a matter of fact that the people, even before the emergence of the Maoists as the single biggest internal security threat, had been trying to address issues of inequalities and injustices, and continue to do so even as the Maoist rebellion is raging. So what was the difference in the government's response prior to the emergence of the Maoists as the 'single biggest threat' and after? Is it not that their emergence as the 'single biggest threat' has forced the government to take the marginalized people a little more seriously? Is it not this that has also given other forms of resistance a sharper profile than what they enjoyed until then? If the Maoists' struggle had no role to play in strengthening other movements, what prevented these non-violent groups from raising their voice against the brutal military suppression of our people for over sixty-six years? Why did they stay mute when thousands were being killed, tortured and disappeared in Kashmir, or when aerial bombings were being launched against the Mizo and the Naga people? How much did these non-violent struggles, for all their protestations about peaceful agitations, contribute in raising the consciousness of the people by campaigning against the 'dirty wars' being fought in India? Consider that in cases like Jammu and Kashmir, it's the armed militancy that gave courage and instilled confidence in people who were beleaguered, and created the condition which persuaded them to think about the need for a mass upsurge to press home the need for a political resolution. Once militancy declined, India's 'good people' fell silent and they forgot all about a democratic solution for the Kashmiris' demand for 'azadi' from a forced union with India. On the other hand, not only has the Maoist armed struggle forced the government to think of the 'poorest of poor', even if hypocritically but has also actually helped non-violent struggles gain leverage. They now leverage the armed struggle of the Maoists to extract concessions from the State. If the armed resistance were to weaken, they would find that they are heard even less by the rulers.

Nevertheless, it is also true that the Maoists place 'war' or the 'politics of bloodshed' as the main means to capture power. So although they fight a war of defence, their political ambition is to overwhelm the Indian ruling classes through PPW. So the question that arises is: aren't they also responsible for the ensuing prosecution of war?

The answer would appear to be in the affirmative except when one looks at it closely, then it becomes more nuanced. Just because some people advocate capture of power through PPW, it does not mean that the initiative was in their hands when they began. It's a long process which has a history starting from 1966 to now, of nearly five decades. Through this period, the demand for democratic agrarian reforms and socially useful forms of employment generation, as well as qualitative improvement in people's lives, was raised by a variety of political formations on the left, particularly the Naxalite movement, which could have undercut the need for waging struggle. It would have thwarted the Maoists from gaining support, mobilizing and organizing themselves, slowly and gradually improving and honing their military skills or in being able to persuade people to join them to fight for their self-preservation. Thus for PPW, a rootedness among people is absolutely imperative. It is this social anchorage in an area being eyed by rapacious mining and industrial corporate houses that has catapulted them into becoming enemy number one of the Indian government. The point is that while both the ruling classes and the revolutionaries need to justify themselves, the task is much more arduous for the Maoists than the State because of the far superior resources available to the State; in the case of the PPW, it gets its force multiplied only if it enjoys the people's support. For the Maoists, it's the quality of their politics and resistance that wins them legitimacy; if they fare poorly on these counts, it can result in an erosion of the social sanction they enjoy.

Therefore, the role played by the CPI (Maoist) is catalytic, especially because in 2004–05 they were dealt a grievous blow in Andhra Pradesh where nearly 1600 of their cadres were killed, arrested or forced to surrender. Soon thereafter, in 2005, came the officially blessed (by the state as well as the Centre) Salwa Judum in Chhattisgarh. No one believed that the Maoists would survive the military onslaught, let alone bounce back from this double blow. Well, they did. So much so that almost all the contemporary social welfare legislations, be it the National Rural Employment Guarantee Act (NREGA), the Forest Rights Act (FRA), the enforcement of Panchayat Extension to Scheduled Areas (PESA), the proposal to form joint forest management committees managed by the gram sabha, have all been inspired or advocated by referring to the need to wean away the poorest among the poor from the Maoists/Naxalites. The refrain has been that were the government to go ahead with their mining projects against the wishes of the Adivasis, then the Adivasis would continue to look upon Maoists as their saviours. Listen to what Jairam Ramesh, the Union Minister for Rural Development, had to say when the Forest Advisory Committee recently cleared the transfer of 500 hectares of land in Jharkhand's Singhbhum Elephant Reserve, to Jindal Steel and Power Ltd. This was done by ensuring that the Gram Sabha permission, deemed mandatory after the passage of the Forest Rights Act, was not required for transferring the land for mining.

> Over the past year, I have been at great pains to counter Maoist propaganda that the Saranda Development Project is a ploy to benefit private mining interests. This Forest Advisory Committee decision is a huge setback and very retrograde.[2]

Why the minister believed his own propaganda is of course a matter of curiosity. But what is not is the fact that it is the Maoists who have been proved right. But much more than this, the turn of events confirms that the surge in war is a step taken by the government to promote and protect the interests of the corporate sector. It is this that lay behind the dilution of FRA by using perfectly legal means. It also means that so long as the Maoists remained in control of the Saranda forest, corporate mining was inconceivable. Now that the Maoists have been forced out and developments in

Saranda pave the way for a corporate takeover, what are India's peace-and system-loving 'good people' going to do to stem this move?

Polemics apart, the point is that when the Maoists appeared robust and strong, the entire resistance gained, and the terms of debate on 'development' and the nature of such 'development' were not lopsided. In contrast, since the Maoists suffered a setback, the terms of debate have shifted, and yet again the issue being posed is how to unleash the 'animal spirit' of capitalism in order to reinvigorate the Indian economy. Thus, so as to blunt the peasant opposition, the tweaking of environmental laws and laws meant to empower the tribal people are foremost on the government agenda. Whether there is a causal relationship or it is a co-relationship or a coincidence (a fortuitous one for the owners of capital) is not so hard to understand because it is only when the Maoists were forced to retreat from Saranda that the Indian military moved in and set up camps; in the meantime, the rights of the forest dwellers were diluted to suit the corporate sector.

Thus the seminal contribution of the CPI (Maoist)-led PPW lies in placing on the agenda not only the issue of the much-needed reforms that tend to improve the life, dignity and liberty of an overwhelming number of people – providing relief especially for the most marginalized – but even more in privileging the need for a politics of transformation through seizure of power. It is this that breathed life back into the movement for revolution and made it part of the public agenda. This is truly phenomenal in so far as the overground communist parties never could inspire or succeed in restoring the seizure of power on to their agenda, because they made a virtue of electoral politics and played down the predatory nature of the Indian State. The Maoists succeeded where others failed because the People's War captured the people's imagination–it has inspired, encouraged and motivated them, while creating fear among the ruling classes, triggering a virulent opposition to the Maoists. It is the PPW that has made people *acutely* sensitive to the issues of land grab, forest displacement, water privatization, malnutrition, and rural employment; the protracted war has acted as a force multiplier for all social and political struggles. The uncovering of this reality has driven the corporate sector into a tailspin because their greed for profit has been thoroughly exposed. Therefore, only the naïve can believe that the weakening of the armed resistance would benefit the overall resistance. On the contrary, if there is something that provides confidence and inspires people to struggle, it is this war. It also acts to restrain the government from carrying out an all-out crackdown on non-violent resistance movements in India because of the fear that more people would then join the Maoist PPW.

Does this mean that we have no choice but to practice the 'politics of bloodshed'? NO. It only means that for anyone to believe that the system can be made 'inclusive' and 'humane' by simply appealing to the enlightened self-interest of the rulers is akin to believing that a government soldier involved in suppressing a popular movement will acutely abide by the fundamentals of human rights. Of course, in the name of inclusiveness a few crumbs would be apportioned, as an act of benevolence, while ensuring that most of it is looted. Consider how the sectors of health and education have become conduits for transferring public funds into private corporations in the name of 'universalizing' these two sectors. For reforms to be reforms, they must be geared towards improving people's lives and liberty, and not be a means for a privileged few to amass more wealth.

In short, it is the PPW that has brought forth to the public agenda the need for revolutionary transformation of India through seizure of political power.

As a result, the Maoists have also raised the bar for the progressive and democratic forces in India. No longer can these forces remain oblivious to the need to challenge conventional wisdom. For this and other reasons, it is time we take PPW seriously, and critically evaluate it.

# I
# In the Beginning There Was War

*If War is an act of force, it belongs necessarily also to the feelings. If it does not originate in the feelings, it reacts, more or less, upon them, and the extent of this reaction depends not on the degree of civilisation, but upon the importance and duration of the interests involved . . . Therefore, if we find civilised nations do not put their prisoners to death, do not devastate towns and countries, this is because their intelligence exercises greater influence on their mode of carrying on War, and has taught them more effectual means of applying force than these rude acts of mere instinct.*

Carl von Clausewitz

Peace is the absence of violence/armed conflict. There is no positive value attached to it per se. Because if such a condition restores tyrannical rule, then it cannot be said to mark progress. It is when the absence of violence helps in the resolution of a dispute, or sets off a process towards resolution, that one valorizes peace. In other words, its specificity and concrete reality determine what it is. War as a cognate of peace is no different. Each war has to be understood in its own specific context. There can be no a priori abstraction which can be imposed on social reality. It is when we study it concretely that war, as much as peace, reveals itself for what it is. To assume that peace is better than war is also a misconception if such a peace crushes human freedom or chains people in bondage or consolidates rapacious rule. Conversely, war is preferred over peace if war is for freeing people from tyrannical rule or it is waged for the removal of the threat of tyranny. There are occasions when war against an occupation force or an aggressor is led by those who, even while they seek to throw off the foreign yoke, end up quashing the freedom and equality of their own people. There are of course occasions when a foreign yoke is sought to be imposed on an independent country using the façade of freeing people from an autocratic rule such as in Libya or that being attempted in Syria. So wars do result in change, except that it could be a change that is not to our liking or not what we prefer. The point is that more than peace, it is war which needs to be explained, analysed and understood. It is when we do it that we discover that wars are and will remain an intrinsic part of social life. What matters is to study it concretely to help us understand what lies behind and what prospects are there to bring it to an end.

There are a great many questions about war or the fear and horror associated with it. But wars have helped resolve and free human beings from enslavement and breathed life into deadlocked situations. With the advantage of hindsight, some may (as indeed some scholars/activists do) dismiss the defeat of French and US imperialism in Indo-China because it paved the way for one-party rule. Some may even feel that the Chinese revolution may have thrown off foreign powers and unified China in order to unchain a billion people without actually freeing them. But that would be like saying that the defeat of fascism paved the way for another form of enslavement (the restoration of colonial rule), and so nothing positive came out of it. But without defeating the fascist powers in a war it would have been difficult to imagine the beginning of the end of the colonial era. The point is also whether war or peace sets into motion a chain of events and helps create conditions which either impede or enable the pursuit of positive resolution. For instance, the end of militancy in Kashmir impeded any progress towards resolution because it was militancy which was privileged and not the people's aspirations. So once militancy seemed to peter off – as the Indian State crushed the militants and restored its authority – it was felt that the movement for 'azadi' itself had lost steam and now there was no pressing need to make any concession. Thus, chances for political resolution appeared better when militancy was strong.

At what point does a problem become so acute as to erupt or develop into violence? Or when are the prospects for political resolution brightest during the course of war? It is when we know these answers that we discover that peace has the capacity to numb good sense and encourage hardliners, especially if one side has an upper hand or advantage. The much-vaunted enlightened self-interest of the rulers does not reveal itself then. So those who clamour for peace often forget that such a condition could be far worse than bloodshed if it ends up crushing a struggle or a movement for justice and freedom. People pretending to be 'peace-loving' can be reactionaries in so far as they uphold the status quo and play by the rules of the establishment.

So what is war? Clausewitz explained it as 'an act of force to compel our enemy to do our will'. A variant of this finds its way into the Indian Army's doctrine of sub-conventional warfare whose objective is 'to transform the will and attitude' of the adversary/enemy. With Clausewitz, we also enter an era when wars between two States, or those between a subjugated people and an imperial State, and those within a State in the form of a civil war, are all acknowledged as different types of war, each to be understood in its own right. But whatever be the definition, and although the nature of war may have changed, there can be little dispute that with Clausewitz, we enter the 'battlefield' of modern warfare. Among other features, the age, nineteenth century, which began with what is considered the first-ever 'People's War' where an entire nation, so to say, rose up in revolt – therefore the Spaniards still call it 'The Spanish War of Independence (1808–14)' – against Napoleon's France, still remains relevant if we look at wars in the twentieth century and the first decade of the twenty-first century. The term 'guerrilla warfare' was used for the first time during the 1808 War and served as a model for the Bolivarian rebellion in Latin America. The great accomplishment of nineteenth-century wars, especially People's War, was

> the renunciation of criminalizing opponents at war, in other words relativizing enmity, the negation of absolute enmity.[3]

The significance of this emerges when we distinguish conventional wars from sub-conventional warfare. The former is a form of warfare where regular armies, of two states or more, fight an all-out war whereas the latter is a form of warfare which takes place among people. Indian Army in its Doctrine of Sub-conventional Operations points out that:

> Total war as an instrument of state policy has become less relevant than ever before and resultantly, the probability of full-scale conventional wars between nations is gradually receding as an option for settling disputes. However, this has given further impetus to sub-conventional operations as the *predominant* form of warfare . . . [it] is a generic term encompassing all armed conflict that are above

> the level of peaceful coexistence amongst states and below the threshold of war. It includes militancy, insurgency, proxy war and terrorism that may be employed as a means in an insurrectionist movement or undertaken independently.[4] [Emphasis added.]

Although the Indian Army doctrine tends to conflate sub-conventional war with the 'proxy war' waged by one State against another (obviously referring to Pakistan and the Kashmir insurgency), the fact is, as their own doctrine later argues, the distinguishing characteristic of such wars is that it takes place amongst people and invariably within the borders of a nation-state. The rebels, therefore, tend to get illegitimized because the nation-state is chary of according recognition to them.

Our era is marked by a further retreat from legitimacy for rebels as they get 'criminalized' and declared 'illegal combatants', devoid of any privileges.[5] But every now and then contrarian developments too take place. Thus, as the present Syrian conflict escalated, the International Committee of Red Cross (ICRC) declared that the country had reached a state of civil war; thereby, ICRC was rendering legitimacy to the anti-government militants. While the project to illegalize combatants is a United States-led NATO idea following 11 September 2001, the push to lend legitimacy to combatants fighting the Syrian government means that this principle has not been abandoned but is being read selectively, privileging some and outlawing others depending on the power equation and stakes of the foreign powers. Thus, whereas Bahrain dissidents are militarily suppressed and Kashmiri militants demonized, Syrian dissidents receive NATO arms. Syrian militias are considered legitimate whereas Lebanese Hizbullah is sought to be criminalized and declared illegitimate. Therefore, if the US-led NATO has not succeeded entirely in their attempt to outlaw rebels/irregulars they dislike, it is because of the strong popular backing that, for instance, Hizbullah enjoys among the Shias of Lebanon. The point is that rebels today have to manoeuvre between legitimacy earned because of popular backing and being designated criminal because they have earned the wrath of the powers-that-be.

It is interesting to note that the progressive development of international laws of war which rendered recognition to rebels/irregulars was accompanied by the criminalizing of rebels by the colonial powers. In this sense, unequal power relations between countries when colonialism predominated, played a role in the co-existence of the progressive laws of war with the most reactionary practices in the colonies. With the emergence of postcolonial nation-states and the consolidation of imperialism, this has persisted under the rubric of terrorism.

Paradoxically, just when 'People's War' gained legitimacy in the nineteenth century, it also coincided with the age when European powers created a mercenary force from among the 'natives' they colonized, which then went on to form the nucleus that protected Europe's rule in these colonies and helped keep the 'natives' subdued/ subservient/suppressed. If at its height, only 75,000 English officers and 1,50,000 native soldiers kept 350 million Indians in bondage, it was because this force served the British Raj loyally. Philip Mason in his classic study of the Indian Army writes that the British Army made 'mercenary' a term of honour.[6] As he observed, it is one thing for a man to work for cash, but he does not die for the sake of cash. That these native soldiers could offer their life for their regimental colours/officers or to protect his platoon was an illustration of the kind of allegiance that soldiers owed to their officers and colleagues; in the bargain, without much demur, they would obey their colonial masters' orders to suppress and persecute their own people.

Thus modern warfare was marked, on the one hand, by the emergence of People's War, and on the other, it was characterized by the raising of a professional/mercenary force which helped maintain alien rule for centuries. But it is also about how guerrilla warfare resulted in great triumphs for revolutionary and national liberation struggles and then lost ground when they seized power, something much of postcolonial world history has grappled with. The other feature of our age is, particularly in India, the relentless wars waged against people by the postcolonial State. The military, which once served alien rulers, shifted allegiance to the native ruling classes. So much so that the warriors of India's freedom struggle, the Indian National Army, were prosecuted by the very same Indian Army which served the British Raj, for waging the war of independence. Postcolonial nation-states have had no moral compunction against using colonial institutions nor have they hesitated in augmenting and using their coercive military power against their own people in much the same way that the colonial powers had done.

Moreover, just as war-making did not end with transfer of power to the native ruling classes, the move to deny a linkage between war and politics too gathered force. A tendency to demonize the opponent, and deny him/her any legitimacy or context, gained ground. One part of the argument is to valorize non-violence to an extent that it becomes something of a religious dogma. The other is to claim that structural violence that can result in killings or a miserable life for millions is less worrisome than political violence. There are some who adopt the statist position which rests on the Weberian advocacy of the State enjoying monopoly over violence and therefore, upholding the State's right to wage war even against its own people, while fanatically rejecting the people's right to offer armed resistance. (Such 'good' people maintain scrupulous silence over the forty million guns in the hands of soldiers, cops, private security and upper class/caste, predominately Hindu males.)

John Keegan rejects the argument that war and politics belong within the 'same continuum'.[7] For him, 'warfare is almost as old as man himself'. He points towards the 'endemic warfare of non-state, even pre-state peoples', which are, according to him, wars 'without beginning or end'. Thus, he also draws a line between the civilized behaviour of the regular soldier and the barbarism of the irregulars. So, is war an independent variable? While wars may have been part of mankind's pre-history and may not have been subordinated to social needs and pressures in those times, to insist that wars in our own times could be a result of something innate and rooted in culture is to deny the political origins of wars.

As a result, the irony escapes Keegan when he contends that:

> [W]orld Community needs . . . skilful and disciplined warriors who are ready to put themselves at the service of its authority. Such warriors must properly be seen as the protectors of civilisation, not its enemies . . . (i.e.) against ethnic bigots, regional warlords, ideological intransigents, common pillagers and organized international criminals.[8]

To be fair, Keegan does not identify any one army as representing the 'skilful and disciplined soldiers' that the world civilization needs. However, barbarism is not something confined to the 'irregulars'. The most advanced and civilized country could wage a savage war whose bestiality could shock the most battle-hardened warriors. The use of aerial bombing by the Allied Forces over Dresden in Germany during the Second World War or the use of nuclear bomb by US against Japan, the use of 'Agent Orange' by US forces in Indo-China, etc., show that savagery is not culture specific. Another feature of savagery is the use of so-called 'irregulars' by the State security forces. These irregulars are soldiers who operate covertly backed by official patronage and sanction. They are deliberately and consciously employed by the regular armies to carry out tasks that they themselves find difficult to perform. Thus, if the Indian security forces employ Salwa Judum, Ikhwanis, SULFAs, Tritya Sammelan Prastuti Committee . . . it is because the depredations of these irregulars benefit the overall calculations of the regular armies. But a word of caution. In reality, there is nothing which suggests that barbarism is peculiar to irregulars—regular armies such as of the US-led NATO or Russia have been as savage in their conduct of wars. The manner in which Indian and Pakistani troops behave also smacks of savagery. Beheading soldiers and killing a captured combatant are not uncommon to them. Some may attribute this to the bitter historical divide between Hindus and Muslims, and their shared history of mutual suspicion.

So to draw a Maginot Line between the regular and the irregular does not always hold. How does one then explain the emergence of ethnic/communal regular armies and the cruel forms of warfare they lapse into? How does one explain the Afghan Taliban fighters? Do they not fit into this divide? Is there no difference between the wars of 'civilized people' and others considered 'uncivilized'?

There would have been but for the fact that even soldiers of regular armies such as those of the Indian Army fight for their platoon and regimental colours, and invoke their religion; it's not the idea of a modern, secular socialist republic that motivates them. Neither the US soldier deployed against the Afghans or Iraqis, nor the Indian soldier suppressing Kashmir's movement for 'azadi' display civilized sensibility when fighting such 'aliens' or the 'other' who is also so demonized that large-scale killing of them neither arouses indignation nor is considered barbaric. On the contrary, what dominates the discourse is the fact that 'civilized' nations applaud and find excuses for such bloodletting.

Therefore, it is an ideological/political positioning that attempts to de-civilize and also criminalize some groups/communities, while glorifying those fighting to suppress them. One is reminded of the recent US-led propaganda, which sought to show everyone else, other than them, as evildoers.

Does this mean that all wars are barbaric? The fact of the matter is that both regular and irregular armies have thrown up examples of barbaric as well as civilized behaviour on the battleground. In India, the Naga underground, a quintessential ethnic irregular army, showed higher morality in its conduct of war, treating humanely the captured soldiers of the Indian military and causing minimal harm to the civilians. Conversely, in the case of the Indian military, we know very well that its soldiers have not shown any compunction in targeting civilians; this began with the Indian military's role in the Hyderabad 'police action' which sought to merge the Nizam-ruled Hyderabad into the Indian Union, and also in the army's operations against the Communist revolutionaries in 1948–51. In the first instance, the Indian Army allowed massacres of Muslims, and engaged in loot and pillage. Of course, this was justified by claiming that the

Nizam's Razakars had been particularly vicious towards the Hindu subjects. At the same time, the army was equally vicious against the peasantry for siding with the Communists. The reason why this feature of war fought by the Indian military never finds any mention or this history is hardly recalled, is because the victorious side plays down its own barbaric acts and plays up those of its opponents.

So, is there no difference between regular and irregular armies and the way they fight wars?

The difference has to do with the failure to distinguish between conventional warfare (mostly between two or more States) and sub-conventional wars (which are marked by being war waged against one's own people). Unlike two State armies fighting each other, 'small wars' take place among the citizens, where they are the main target of the State forces. It is this genre of war that shows greater propensity towards barbarism compared to the conventional genre.

The difference between two armies fighting a conventional war and guerrillas fighting counter-guerrillas also shows that war as a continuation of *policy* differs from war as a continuation of *politics.* War between States can loosely be characterized as a policy, whereas war against the State's own people is a continuation of politics. Mary Kaldor concurs with this when she argues that policy relates to 'relations to other states, and politics as the domestic process of mediating different interests and views'.[9] Although it ought to be kept in mind that policy too flows out of politics.

When Indian opinion-makers argue that to bring Pakistan on board, India will have to make every effort to create an environment whereby Islamabad feels encouraged to develop some stakes in friendly relations with India or '*is compelled to do so by raising the cost of enmity and conflict*', it is a policy approach being proposed. When Indian observers insist that the government employ harsher means against the Maoists 'in the interest of the State', it reveals class politics. It is also significant that the political narrative of warring parties, with each side justifying their position, also act as a technique for political mobilization, polarizing 'us' and 'them', thereby helping forge bonds. In this sense too, war cannot cease being a continuation of politics – one in which culture and historical context do influence the course of events. For instance, the Indian State's response to the Kashmiri insurgency or the Naga insurgency was overlaid with a heavy dose of cultural disdain towards ethnic and religious minorities, and with hostility towards Pakistan and China.

What is striking is the fact that fewer wars in the twenty-first century are fought around some universal principle (like in the case of anti-imperialist wars and wars of national liberation in Indo-China, Korea and Cuba); mostly it has to do with the exclusivist and the particularistic. Ironically, it is imperialism that wages wars for some universal principle placing a veil over its real motives, which could be for strategic advantage or for securing control over resources considered vital. Contemporary wars in Libya and Syria show how underneath the ostensible democratic upsurge to overthrow a dictatorship, the political narratives could not hide the narrow, particularistic nature of sub-conventional/low intensity wars patronized and financed by the imperialist powers. The religious and sectarian divide as well as the bigotry is all too evident. It is also marked by the fact that the US-led NATO-EU has emerged as the single-biggest practitioner of turning these low-intensity wars into proxy wars to install client/malleable regimes, as well as to wage wars of aggression against other people, as in Afghanistan and Iraq.

Many argue that there is an inner nature of war that logically takes one towards 'Absolute War' meant to defeat the opponent and subject it to the victor's 'will'. The fate of LTTE in Sri Lanka or the vanquishing of Saddam Hussein and Muammar Gaddafi exemplifies this. All three wars reveal features of barbarism in the course of fighting an absolute war. However, Clausewitz has cautioned against ignoring the fluid nature of war, which gets influenced by a variety of factors and can bring about a situation where war gets regulated/contained or brought to a negotiated end. Similarly, wars that were envisaged for a short duration can get stretched for years on end, as it happened between Iran and Iraq in the 1980s. In the current time, the Syrian civil war—which has become a sort of proxy war between Syrians supported by the US-led NATO and its client regimes in West Asia, pitched against the Syrian regime backed by Russia and China—shows how a total war which seemed the most likely course gets toned down due to a military stalemate, forcing an increased effort to find a diplomatic solution. So there is nothing intrinsic in war that defies its containment.

The war in Afghanistan again points towards how a war that began in 2001 to militarily finish Taliban/Al-Qaeda, and bring about a regime change, shifted from absolute to regulated war, and moved towards a negotiated end. The US-led NATO forces now acknowledge that they have failed to subdue the Taliban and that they would much rather retire hurt than persist with an expensive war that has seen the Taliban re-emerge as a military force to reckon with. Meanwhile, it is the alliance between NATO and the Afghan government forces that is unravelling. Consider this from a story filed by an embedded reporter:

> The American side of Dash-e-Top is separated from the Afghan side by a tall wall and a door that can be

> opened only with a code which the Afghans do not have access to. Whereas a close partnership between coalition and Afghan forces, for years considered a cornerstone of the overall military strategy (*shohna ba shohna* – shoulder to shoulder went the ubiquitous NATO slogan), has given way to the Americans distancing and even sequestering themselves from their erstwhile comrades. The about face is a response to insider or 'green on blue' stacks that killed more than 60 foreign troops in 2012 (and wounded 94), accounting for 22 per cent of all coalition combat deaths. Whatever their provenance, the attacks have eroded trust to such a degree that NATO has begun designating some personnel as 'guardian angels'. It is the guardian angel's job to protect the NATO soldier from the Afghan soldier whom it is the NATO soldier's job to train.[10]

And American advisers are now asking their Afghan allies to dismantle many of the military check-posts; however, the Hamid Karzai government fears that this will allow Taliban a free run over the vacated territory.

Thus, every war must also be understood in its specific context wherein external and internal factors can impact its progress.

However, it cannot be denied that national liberation wars, which had once won solidarity and support of world people because of their universalist appeal and vision of a progressive future, have been replaced by particularistic wars which receive less and less popular support because of the absence of a universalist political narrative, say, of fighting colonialism and for independence and social justice, or these can easily become divisive and erode generation of support. Unlike the wars in Indo-China, the one fought by the Afghan Talibans invoking religion or religious persecution have not inspired the world people to rally to their support. On the other side, the number of revolutionary wars has declined, and is today confined to few spots such as Colombia, Philippines and India.

What does this signify? Is revolutionary warfare fast becoming a thing of the past? Or has there been a decline in revolutionary transformation projects? The jury is still out on this, because it cannot be denied that the weakening of the world socialist movement did result in the emergence and proliferation of identity-based struggles. In that sense, it could be argued that this is a temporary and not an absolute change from old forms of war to new ones. Because even in the twentieth century, which saw a proliferation of national liberation struggles, ethnic or particularistic struggles were not absent. The equation may have changed and today revolutionary wars may be few and far between but what is remarkable is that whereas national liberation and revolutionary wars may have declined, *wars as such have not.*

# 2
# War against People

I am concerned here with the genre of warfare that takes place amidst people where culture does rear its head in terms of influencing policies and politics. Soldiers engaged in the suppression of the Kashmiri people's struggle for their right to self-determination saw themselves fighting a proxy war launched by Pakistan, thus conditioning the soldiers to believe that when they were suppressing the Kashmiri Muslims, they were actually fighting Pakistan. The deep-seated hatred for Pakistan, nurtured through propaganda, part of India's popular culture, colours the understanding of these soldiers. Thus when the officers briefed/exhorted their soldiers to fight Kashmiris, they were asking their units to realize that they were actually fighting Pakistan, the most hated enemy. Little to wonder then that these soldiers had little compunction in carrying out a brutal suppression of Kashmiri Muslims.

Be that as it may. There is a difference between the Low Intensity Conflict (LIC) fought by the State and by the guerrillas belonging to a revolutionary movement or for that matter the guerrillas fighting a war against military occupation or those fighting a war against a dictatorship. But before getting there, it is worth noting that very little social science research is devoted to war and analysis of war in India, and those which are being undertaken by a few strategic institutes have not advanced our understanding of the war(s) being fought by the Indian State against its own people; they have also not furthered our understanding about its political dynamics. Indeed, much of the research into stress and trauma, suicides and fraggings, remain outside of the public domain and mostly circulates on a 'need-to-know' basis. The issue of humiliation and terror associated with counter-insurgency and the ethics of waging war against one's own people has not been taken seriously. The issues of class interest, jingoism and Hindutva chauvinism, too, have been ignored. Similarly, no studies have been carried out on how wars waged by the ruling classes further the capitalist landlord interests, and how these wars contribute to the spread of majoritarian communalism, while also are reflective of a Brahminical upper-caste bias. And yet, the very social composition of the Armed Forces of the Union raises such concerns.

The confusion between conventional and sub-conventional wars, the fact that wars against people in post-colonial nation-states are not even recognized as wars/armed conflict, the criminalizing of opponents, etc., all contribute to drawing a veil over them. The one that comes closest to the issue in Indian scholarship is the subject matter of 'militarization', 'militarism', or violence versus non-violence, etc. It is also unfortunate that there is an a priori rejection of war, which forms the premise of the critics of 'militarization' and political violence; this is because of a lack of comprehension about the asymmetrical nature between the power of the State and that of the rebel/partisan. It is equally based on ignorance about the postcolonial State's propensity to wage war against its own people; this, compounded by the critics' disdain for violence results, in practical terms, to acquiescing in wars prosecuted by the Indian State. While a simulated concern for people is embodied in the demand to repeal the AFSPA (although 'repeal' now has been replaced by attempts to 'humanize' AFSPA), it ignores the fact that it is because the Indian State has the propensity to launch wars against its own people that it requires indemnity for its soldiers through Acts like AFSPA. And it has also got to be noted that such impunity will reign supreme even when AFSPA is withdrawn.

Thus, instead of protesting against wars launched by the Indian State, many spend more time calling for revoking or repealing AFSPA, implying that they have nothing against the State launching wars against its own people. The concern expressed by most is that AFSPA indemnifies the Armed Forces of the Union and so prevents prosecution of offenders. This is a somewhat lazy approach to the question of war and peace; this has meant that analysts are loath to actually understand how impunity gets created and how even if AFSPA is removed, the unwillingness to protest against the State's war against its own people, creates virtually the same kind of immunity. Thus, even if AFSPA is repealed, the war-making reflexes of the Indian State will not fade away, and the prospects of democratic resolution of problems and disputes will still be negligible; as an example, take the case of the nine states where Operation Greenhunt is on. And impunity flows not just out of a body of law(s) but also out of the institutions of the State, especially the administration and the judiciary, providing succour to the perpetrators and a cold shoulder to the victims. When the Supreme Court says that every armed force personnel would be presumed to be working in good faith and that this presumption cannot be 'dislodged' by the courts without the government allowing the court to take cognizance of the prima facie evidence, or when the apex court upheld that an armed force personnel would be considered to be on 'active duty' twenty-four hours a day because the BSF Act allows the Central government to simply issue a notification declaring so, then the source of impunity is not just AFSPA.[11] While this provision of being on 'active duty' twenty-four hours protects the soldier's full benefits if injured or killed, it also protects him against prosecution by a civilian court for any crime he commits at any time of the day. Thus, while the prosecution of criminal soldiers becomes a rarity, the soldiers are also extended the incentive to earn reward and promotion by capturing and/or killing suspects and civilians, meaning, they are being encouraged to carry out 'kills' for cash and career improvement. So the rot runs much deeper.[12]

The other aspect is that the Indian State refuses to acknowledge that it is engaged in a prosecution of war inside India, and pretends that it is only undertaking 'police action'. Denying the fact that there are several internal armed conflicts going on in the country, the Indian government has been insisting that these are just 'law and order problems'. Instead of condemning the Indian government for denying the reality of these wars against our own people and the State's refusal to adhere to the minimum ethical norms set by the Geneva Conventions, the Indian analysts/commentators have been ignorant or indifferent to such issues, thereby helping the Indian State escape protests and probe at home. Attack after attack on children and women, schools and clinics run by Maoists or killing of children by claiming that they were Maoist combatants – all these are possible because there is neither intellectual honesty to accept that the Indian State is engaged in a 'dirty war' nor is there appreciation for the need to demand compliance with the Geneva Conventions and Protocols.

Besides, in India, the same people who are passionate in their defence of women's rights and secularism also happen to be the most strident in their denunciation of every movement in the country which picks up arms, while remaining conspicuously silent when faced with charges of rape, massacre, and enforced disappearances levelled against the State forces. India's Kashmir war brings out how, barring honourable exceptions, the democratic-minded intelligentsia and its women's and civil liberties movement have been conspicuously absent throughout the phase of war, instead finding succour in their conviction that the Indian State is somehow better than the rebels who are seen as being Islamic fundamentalists. They are loath to even take up the issue of rape which has been used as a deliberate policy in Kashmir. Till recently, none of these groups have protested on the streets in India or have mobilized opinion against this war in Kashmir. If they have woken up to it now or are now researching into issues concerning sexual violence during armed conflict, it is a moot question if this is being done to sow divisions among the victim population – by pitting women's experience against that of men because such scholarship tends to be hostile/ antipathetic towards the 'azadi' movement – or because of a commitment to rectify the wrongs of the past.

Amidst this reality, the presence of revolutionary movement and revolutionary warfare in present-day India deserves to be taken seriously. It is notable that this movement is considered the 'single biggest source of internal security threat'. This is the official explanation for a war which is passed off as 'police action'. But such semantic subterfuge is part of warfare elsewhere too.

For instance, after the Somalia debacle (where first the UN and then the US-led forces suffered massive losses), the UN formulated a 'duty to protect', doctrine for the so-called victims of authoritarian rule anywhere on earth. Over the past decade, military interventions have gone beyond 'national interest', 'humanitarian relief' and 'duty to protect' to an assumed 'duty' to take up arms against any dictator. Today, any insurgency that can muster an international backing, such as in Libya or that being attempted in Syria, has been able to acquire legitimacy. Thus, some wars are considered all right and others not, depending on the line of support, or rather, which big power alliance is backing which side. But most remarkably, there is no sign of peace-mongering.

Moreover, the actual conduct of war is also undergoing some change. For instance, from a computer console thousands of miles away, and flying a drone looking at a target for hundreds of hours, a combatant can fire missiles.[13]

An editorial in *Hindustan Times* claimed that according to studies, 20-30 per cent civilian casualties have taken place due to drone attacks.[14] 'This', said the edit, 'is low given the nature of the war and compared to traditional aerial bombing or strafing. By any standard of just war drones are morally sound. They are proportionate.' But as drones become more sophisticated and small, easy to carry, especially non-guided drones, which can be carried in backpacks, they would become 'commonplace'. There is nothing to stop even guerrillas from acquiring and carrying drones. So just as Hamas – despite Gaza being virtually cut off from the world and suffering Israeli attacks – could in a single day fire 900 missiles which penetrated the so-called shield that Israel has built to disable rockets before they hit their target, even drones could become a popular tool for guerrillas in the coming years. One wonders if the acolytes of drones would then continue to find them 'morally sound' or would they cry foul?

The founders of Marxism were also pretty well aware of the changing character of war. Engels in his introduction to Karl Marx's *The Class Struggles in France: 1848–1850*, written in 1895, mentions that history has shown that the mode of struggle of 1848 is 'today obsolete in every respect'. And that 'the common form of all these revolutions was that they were minority revolutions'. As a rule, after the 'first great success, the victorious minority divided: one half satisfied with what had been gained, the other wanted to go still further'. Thus:

> [A]lready in 1849 . . . the bourgeoisie had thrown in its lot with the government's, 'culture and property' had hailed and feted the military moving against insurrection. The spell of the barricade was broken; the soldier no longer saw behind it 'the people', but rebels, agitators, plunderers, levelers, the scum of society; the officer had in the course of time become versed in the tactical forms of street fighting, he no longer marched straight ahead and without covers against the improvised breastwork, but went round it through gardens, yards and houses.

He remarked that momentous changes had taken place:

> [T]owns had become larger (Paris and Berlin growing fourfold since 1848) and their garrisons grew even faster which could, with the help of railways, be augmented many fold in reduced time: doubled in 24 hrs and four times in 48 hrs. Guns had improved from smooth bore, muzzle loading percussion gun to small caliber, breech loading magazine rifle which shot four times as far, ten times as accurately and ten times as fast as the former.

On the other side, Engels said that conditions for insurrection have grown worse, that people would appear divided because the middle strata would never 'group round the proletariat'.[15]

But Engels was cautious. This did not mean, he said, that in the future street fighting would no longer play any role, but that since 1848, the conditions had become unfavourable for 'civil fighters and far more favourable for the military'. He also cautioned that 'it will occur more seldom in the beginning of a great revolution than its further progress, and will have to be undertaken with greater forces'. He drew attention to the fact that

> [i]f the conditions have changed in the case of war between nations, this is no less true in the case of the class struggle. The time of surprise attacks, of revolution carried through by small conscious minorities at the head of unconscious masses, is past. Where it is a question of a complete transformation of the social organization, the masses themselves must also be in it, must themselves already have grasped what is at stake, what they are going in for, body and soul.[16]

The point is that each time the war machinery advances and a new generation of weapons enter the scene, warnings are sounded that wars, or rather armed resistance, are becoming redundant. Here, mention has to be made about how the AK-47 rifles revolutionized resistance by providing the guerrillas with a rifle which was durable and easy to dismantle, clean and repair; as a result, resistance received a boost. The proliferation of this weapon and its easy availability has acted to boost the morale of the resistance fighters. The point is not to glorify wars by showing how technological advancement helps to enable wars but to point out that technological advancement actually trickles down much faster than trickle-down economic theory.

However, the biggest shift in war is now the role and the preponderance of mercenaries, euphemistically called 'private security services', in the actual conduct of wars being fought by the States. *The Economist* recently claimed that 'soldiers-for-hire' is a business worth 100 billion dollars. And these security services are not bound by any regulation or code of conduct. In India, private security services reportedly employ no less than a million 'armed security guards'. Most of the security services used by the industrial conglomerates employ ex-servicemen, i.e., trained soldiers, not only to secure the plant and equipment but actually to control and discipline the workforce. When Maruti Suzuki reopened its Manesar unit after a lockout, they did so after recruiting 100 ex-soldiers and deploying them on the floor, thus making it clear that they were there to keep an eye on the workers. Reliance India Ltd (RIL) has a private armed force a few thousands in number, ostensibly to protect its plants. Its security advisors include an ex-army chief and an ex-DG of police; other corporate houses too have increased their recruitment of ex-army officers so as to raise their own company forces. Why private companies are allowed to raise their own armed force is one issue. The other is that it is not as though the state police or paramilitary forces are inimically disposed towards the industrial conglomerates. They are always there to do the bidding of the owners of capital. In Jharkhand's Saranda forest, nineteen camps of CRPF are coming up in an area to protect the mining concessions granted to loot the iron ore deposits from the area. In Raogarh district, the State-owned Bhilai Steel Plant is spending Rs 5000 crore to pay for raising a special Central Industrial Security Force contingent to protect its iron ore mines. In fact, the CISF provides private corporations its trained soldiers as guards to their plants, and also as personal security staff, for a price. (Infosys was the first beneficiary of this CISF offer and paid Rs 27 lakh per month for 101 soldiers. RIL pays CISF Rs 34 lakh per month for providing 217 personnel.) The extent of firepower that the ruling class has today to do its bidding is staggering.

In such circumstances, it would be unrealistic to rule out armed struggle.

# 3

# 'Vein of Prudery'

Now, among one of the several reasons for the lack of appreciation of war, and its virtual absence from the debates of the academia – and thus the Indian democratic movement's inability to even progress beyond the demand for repeal of AFSPA – has to do with the blind spot of the Left Movement in India. It has no answer to questions such as: What is the place of war within the general Marxist theory of society? Is war an independent variable or does Clausewitz's thesis of war as continuation of politics/ policies hold good in the twenty-first century? What does the Indian State's wars against its own people say about the character and nature of the Indian State?

There is, for one, no Marxist theory of war. What compounds the problem is the 'vein of political prudery' in Marxist scholarship where the matter of war and its role, if not continued relevance, for revolutionary transformation, is concerned.[17] Engels has more published writings on matters of military compared to all other subjects. Marx had written extensively on wars. One of his memorable writings was on 'Revolutionary Spain' which he wrote for *New York Daily Tribune* in 1854. A remarkable piece was on 'Guerrilla Warfare', which dealt with the period of Spanish resistance against Napoleon's army, 1808–14, whose lessons, as Marx then wrote, still appears relevant when analysing what had by then come to be accepted as a new genre of war, namely, People's War using guerrilla warfare, and examining it critically for its shortcomings but taking the war itself seriously.

> By comparing the three periods of guerrilla warfare with the political history of Spain, it is found that they represent the respective degrees into which the counter-revolutionary spirit of the Government had succeeded in cooling the spirit of the people. Beginning with the rise of whole populations, the partisan war was next carried on by guerrilla bands, of which whole districts formed the reserve and terminated in *corps francs* continually on the point of dwindling into banditti, or sinking down to the level of standing regiments.
>
> Estrangement from the Supreme Government, relaxed discipline, continual disasters, constant formation, decomposition, and recomposition during six years of the *cadrez* must have necessarily stamped upon the body of the Spanish army the character of praetorianism, making them equally ready to become the tools or the scourges of their chiefs. The generals themselves had necessarily participated in, quarrelled with, or conspired against the Central Government, and always thrown the weight of their sword into the political balance. Thus Cuesta, who afterwards seemed to win the confidence of the Central Junta at the same rate that he lost the battles of the country, had begun by conspiring with the *Consejo Real* and by arresting the Leonese deputies to the Central Junta. General Morla himself, a member of the Central Junta, went over into the Bonapartist camp, after he had surrendered Madrid to the French. The coxcombical Marquis de las Romerias, also a member of the Junta, conspired with the vainglorious Francisco

> Palafox, the wretched Montijo, and the turbulent Junta of Seville against it. The Generals Castaños, Blake, La Bisbal (an O'Donnell) figured and intrigued successively at the times of the Cortes as regents, and the Captain-General of Valencia, Don Javier Elío, surrendered Spain finally to the mercies of Ferdinand VII. The praetorian element was certainly more developed with the generals than with their troops.
>
> On the other hand, the army and guerrilleros which received during the war part of their chiefs, like Porlier, Lacy, Eroles and Villacampa, from the ranks of distinguished officers of the line, while the line in its turn afterward received guerrilla chiefs, like Mina, Empecinado, etc. were the most revolutionized portion of Spanish society, recruited as they were from all ranks, including the whole of the fiery, aspiring and patriotic youth, inaccessible to the soporific influence of the Central Government; emancipated from the shackles of the ancient regime; part of them, like Riego, returning after some years' captivity in France. We are, then, not to be surprised at the influence exercised by the Spanish army in subsequent commotions; neither when taking the revolutionary initiative, nor when spoiling the revolution by praetorianism.

It is worth noting that both Marx and Engels wrote on several wars in their own times such as the American Civil War, Bismarck's wars, the First War of Independence in India, or the suppression of the Paris Commune, etc. Engels, on the other hand, prided himself on being something of an expert on military matters having participated in his youth in military action, and in his own social circle he was nicknamed 'general'. Engels's contribution was more pronounced also because it was his genius that promoted for German Social Democrats a new vision of military preparedness based on a small professional army that was recruited, with the underlying assumption that the German working class and its party were the 'party of national defence'. The electoral successes with the achievement of universal suffrage gave the German Social Democracy to believe that the German working class was a stakeholder and therefore they also accepted that the German State was as much theirs as it was of the exploiting classes.

This apart, both Marx and Engels favoured some wars and opposed others. Wars which were seen as accelerating social change were regarded as playing a progressive role. Marx and Engels, in particular, took Clausewitz seriously (reference to Clausewitz in their own writings testifies to this) and found close commonality of concerns arising from Clausewitz's insistence that war 'is not an activity of the will exerted upon inanimate matter . . . but against a living and re-acting force' and therefore belongs to the 'province of social life'.

The 'triumph' of Bismarck's militarism, and the 'suppression' of the Paris Commune, found Marx and Engels turning their attention to war preparation among the European powers; they started working to forestall the outbreak of a 'world' war. For Engels, the possibility of a world war was deeply disturbing for he feared both the destruction which could be wreaked as well as that such a war 'would set . . . jingoism going everywhere . . .' [18] No longer was Engels unequivocal in locating the opportunities arising out of the impending war for revolutionary transformation. The ambiguity in Marxism over war draws much on these anxieties about world war and the fear of jingoism expressed by Engels, but these concerns directly addressed the challenges posed to the socialists in Europe.

Gilbert Achcar draws attention to the fact that both Marx and Engels did not concern themselves so much with what politics a particular war was the continuation of as with the question 'what underlying historical movement it was the bearer of'.[19] Engels in particular was concerned about the Franco-Prussian war (1870) degenerating into a war against the French people. By 1887, he was warning of a world war in which more than 810 million combatants would be engaged and cause destruction and raise chauvinism. Engels feared that in the event of a world war only barbarism would be certain, not the victory of socialism.

It is here that the seminal contributions of Lenin and then Mao make their mark. They found in Clausewitz's writings insights that help conceptualize revolutionary warfare. Guerrilla war for Clausewitz, as for other reformers in his circle in the early nineteenth-century Prussia, was 'preeminently a political matter in the highest sense of the word, of an almost revolutionary character'. The very emergence of 'guerrilla warfare' was a recognition of this new form of war called 'People's War'. The creative application of his theory to the concrete reality of a Russia or a China is what revolutionized the Marxist thinking on war. But it was Lenin and then Mao who took the idea of 'War as a Political Instrument' and found it compatible with their project of revolutionary transformation. The question of treating war as a continuation of politics is beyond doubt where 'Low Intensity Warfare' is concerned.

Clausewitz's writings on the role of partisans/irregulars could be meshed with the armed Communist revolution. While war as 'continuation of politics' applied to all wars, the political character of war, nevertheless, determined whether it was to be an 'Absolute War' or a 'Real War'.[20] The idea of Absolute War, aimed at 'disarming or destruction of the enemy . . . or the threat of this' destruction was read with Marxist class war through what Clausewitz defined as 'absolute enmity'. Thus, in both war and politics, identifying and choosing of friends and enemies, deciding on absolute enmity versus relative enmity and therefore, real war in which war could be contained or regulated, became of critical importance. When Mao said that 'politics is war without bloodshed while war is politics by bloodshed', he was suggesting that politics is a continuum.[21] Carl Schmitt points out that what Lenin learned from Clausewitz

> was not just the famous formula of war as the continuation of politics. It involved the recognition that in the age of revolution the distinction between friend and enemy is the primary distinction, decisive for war as for politics. Only revolutionary war is true war for Lenin, because it derives from absolute enmity. Everything else is a conventional game.

Lenin pointed towards another feature of war, something which Engels too had foreseen as happening in Europe as clouds of war gathered; Lenin wrote in *Bellicose Militarism and the Anti-Militarist Tactics of Social Democracy* (1908) that the bourgeois governments could declare a war 'specially calculated to arouse patriotic and chauvinist feelings among wide sections of the population' in order to isolate or weaken resistance. He also recalled Kautsky to point out that it was often quite impossible to make out

> especially at times of patriotic excitement whether a particular war has been brought about with defensive or aggressive aims . . . Social democrats may find themselves even in a position to demand offensive wars.[22]

Thus, for Lenin it is not the defensive or the offensive character of wars but the interests of class struggle that represents the sole criterion for considering and deciding the attitude. And he quotes Rosa Luxembourg to say that

> interests of the capitalist states and the interests of the proletariat in foreign policy are opposed to one another . . . if militarism is the offspring of capitalism then wars too cannot be abolished by the intrigues of rulers and diplomats; and the task of socialists is not to awaken illusions on this score, but on the contrary constantly expose the hypocrisy and impotence of diplomatic 'peaceful démarches'.[23]

In a review of Engels's *Notes on War*, a collection of sixty articles, reprinted from the *Pall Mall Gazette 1870–71*, Leon Trotsky wrote that

> [o]nly very naïve persons can think that the greatness of a Marx, Engels, or Lenin consists in the automatic infallibility of all their judgments. No, they too made mistakes. But in judging the greatest and the most complicated questions they used to make fewer mistakes than all the others . . . [T]heir mistakes, when the reasons for them are seriously examined, often proved to be deeper and more instructive than the correct judgment of those who, accidentally or not, were right as against them in this or that case.

And proceeded to state:

> [O]ne of the fundamental philosophical premises of Marxism says that truth is always concrete. This means that the profession of war and its problems cannot be dissolved into social and political categories. War is war, and the Marxist who wants to judge it must bear in mind that the truth of war is also concrete.

Therefore, the merit of Engels consisted in the fact that

> while he had profound grasp of the independent character of war – with its own inner technique, structure, its methods, traditions and prejudices – she

> was at the same time a great expert in politics, to which war is in the last analysis subordinated.

He concludes by saying

> this revolutionary interest in war questions, as, moreover, in many other questions, was almost completely lost. But opportunism was perhaps most plainly expressed in the superficial and disdainful attitude toward militarism as a barbaric institution unworthy of enlightened social democratic attention. The war (1914–18) took the socialist parties by surprise and converted their formally oppositional attitude towards militarism into humble genuflections.[24]

In other words, there can be no a priori rejection of war, especially guerrilla war, nor an elevation of war to occupy centrality to the exclusion of all other forms of struggle. But the need is to see war as a continuum of politics/policies and to analyse it concretely.

However, while Lenin's and Mao's exposition on revolutionary warfare are important, John Keegan's plea for 'intellectual restraint' and for subordinating the 'warrior impulse' actually points towards trying to prevented, if it can be prevented, the prosecution of war, or when war breaks out, to regulate and contain it. This is unexceptionable and fits in with attempts at containing war(s), even sub-conventional ones, so that a war is prevented from escalating into the pursuit of a total or absolute war. In short, before a military-solution approach prolongs and transforms the war, it is brought to an end through negotiations. Then the question arises: If negotiations result in disadvantageous terms for one party and advantageous ones for the other, would such a course be sustainable? Will not conflict ensue? There is nothing inevitable, because the point is that the outcome cannot be predicted, predicated as it is on what happens on the battlefront: Is it a military stalemate or has one side emerged with gains and the other suffered losses? In other words, while moving to avoid an absolute war, it is not as though it will be easy to bring it to an end where all sides feel contented. It may as well become a prelude to unleashing war at a later date. Nevertheless, what is important is to take war, especially revolutionary war, and its conduct and consequence, seriously. That is where revolutionaries have to recognize the importance of gaining legitimacy. Legitimacy for revolutionaries is an imperative, which they can scarcely ignore, and they have to fight in order to earn it. The unequal power relations between the forces of the government and the rebels, as well as the asymmetrical nature of warfare, which takes place among the people, underline the need for gaining legitimacy. It becomes essential, in a situation where the government demonizes the rebels as criminals so as to deny them any recognition as a political force since they are projected as being enemies, terrorists/anarchists, the rebels have to constantly struggle against this projected image to remain a legitimate political force.

# 4
# Revolutionary Warfare

Lenin, in the opening words of his 1906 essay on 'Guerilla Warfare', insists that Marxism does not bind the socialist movement to any one particular form of struggle. 'Marxism demands an absolute historical examination of the question of the forms of struggle.' Addressing frontally the opponents of guerrilla warfare, he opined:

> [I]t is not guerilla actions which disorganize the movement but the weakness of a party which is incapable of taking such actions under its control. That is why the anathemas which we Russians usually hurl against guerilla actions go hand in hand with secret, casual and unorganized guerilla action which really do disorganize the Party. Being incapable of understanding what historical conditions give rise to this struggle, we are incapable of neutralizing its deleterious aspects . . . Our complaints against guerilla warfare are complaints against our Party's weakness in the matter of uprising.

But he goes on to argue that '[t]he question, however, is whether the enmity can be contained and regulated, that is, whether it represents relative or absolute enmity'.[25] Therefore, the issue is 'about the quantitative proportion of military action to be conducted by a regular army relative to other methods of class warfare that are not openly military'. Mao finds an exact number: 'revolutionary war is ninth-tenths non-open, non-regular war, and just one-tenth open military war'.[26] Che was more lyrical when he wrote that

> combat is the most important drama in the guerrilla's life. It occupies only a short time; but nevertheless these stellar moments acquire an extraordinary importance, since each small encounter is a battle of fundamental kind for the combatant.[27]

However, wars are not just 'politics by other means', war is also politics where they leave their impact not by what causes them but by their *result* and knowing that war in its aim, method and intensity changes as it proceeds.[28] So war as a continuum of politics and the specific nature of each war made perfect sense to Lenin.

Mao develops this further when he says that

> military action is a method used to attain a political goal. While military affairs and political affairs are not identical, it is impossible to isolate one from the other . . . There are political activities first as applied to the troops; second as applied to the people; and third as applied to the enemy . . . With guerillas, a discipline of compulsion is ineffective. In any revolutionary army, there is unity of purpose as far as both officers and men are concerned, and, therefore, within an army, discipline is self-imposed . . . In a revolutionary army, all individuals enjoy political liberty and the question for example of the emancipation of the people must be not only be tolerated but discussed, and propaganda must be encouraged. Further . . . the mode of living of the officers and the soldiers must not differ too much and this is particularly true in the case of guerilla troops.[29]

In other words, politics permeates revolutionary wars. Or at least that is what needs to be cultivated and imbibed. Military action is a method used to attain a political goal. While military affairs and political affairs are not identical, it is impossible to isolate one from the other.

Mao quotes Lenin on 'Guerilla Warfare' (1906) as saying:

> It is necessary to be completely unsympathetic to abstract formulas and rules and to study with sympathy the conditions of the actual fighting, for these will change in accordance with the political and economic situations and the realization of the people's aspirations. These progressive changes in conditions create new methods.[30]

Thus, conduct of warfare does not remain unaffected by other factors. And Mao distinguished between two types of guerrilla warfare: revolutionary guerrilla warfare based on the masses and where guerrillas are organized into units. The other is guerrilla units that oppress the masses. Therefore, he points out that 'while guerrillas have bases their primary field of activity is in enemy's rear. They themselves have no rear'. Whereas orthodox armies may, due to change in situation, function as guerrillas temporarily, it is also true that guerrilla units may gradually develop into regular units and employ orthodox mobile war.

But partisan war becomes 'a politically charged phrase', because in a revolutionary war 'adherence to a revolutionary party implies nothing less than total integration [Erassung]. Other groups and associations and the state in its current form, are no longer able to integrate their members and adherents so totally as a revolutionary party does its active fighters'. [31] Thus, the motivation and calibre of the personnel who actually fight is of importance.

Mao points out:

> In all armies obedience of the subordinates to their superiors must be exacted. This is true in case of guerrilla discipline, but the basis for guerrilla discipline must be the individual conscience. With guerrillas a discipline of compulsion is ineffective... Discipline is self-imposed.[32]

Thus there is a seminal difference between how discipline is exacted in a professional/mercenary army where people work for salary and serve as employee, and a guerrilla force in which people volunteer their services without a salary because they identify with the movement and its goal. In the case of a professional army, desertion and refusal to fight during battles can invite stringent punishment, including death, but such a stricture cannot be imposed by a guerrilla army where discipline is self-imposed.

In another perceptive observation, Mao went on to stress that

> [i]n a revolutionary army all individuals enjoy political liberty and the question, for example, of the emancipation of the people must not only be tolerated but discussed and propaganda must be encouraged. Furthermore in such an army the mode of living of the officers and the soldiers must not differ too much, and this is particularly true in the case of guerilla troops. Officers should live under the same conditions as their men, for that is the only way in which they can gain from their men the admiration and confidence so vital in war . . . there must be equality of existence in accepting the hardships and dangers of war, thus we may attain the unification of the officer and soldier . . . a unity both horizontal within the group itself and vertical that is from lower to higher echelons.[33]

And he warns that

> [i]t is only undisciplined troops who make the people their enemies and who like the fish out of its native element cannot live.[34]

It is worth noticing that he was drawing attention to the nature of the politics practised by the revolutionary soldiers as not being different but also imbued with political values.

What is the difference between a government soldier and a rebel one? In the Indian context, what propels people to join the Armed Forces of the Union? There are both pull and push factors. If the push factor is poor employment generation in rural as well as urban areas and/or non-availability of jobs, the pull factors are the burgeoning growth in employment generation in the Armed Forces of the Union compared to other branches of the government, and at a time when the majority of the working people put in long hours, receive poor pay and benefits and are denied any right to form unions because the short-term nature of employment of contract and construction workers acts as an impediment to their fighting for their rights. A study of the first volume of the Expenditure Budget of the Government of India over the years reveals that whereas employment generation is either negative in different government departments or growth is negligible, manpower augmentation in the Armed Forces has carried on unabated. This is one area which has been more or less immune to the problems of deficit, inflations, and scarcity of resources. For instance, in 2010 the Central paramilitary forces numbered 8,66,369. In 2011 they rose to 9,13,801, in 2012 to 9,51,464, in 2013, it is 10,07,966, and in 2014, it will be 10,36,974. The army is pushing to raise a new mountain corps as well as two new divisions plus an armoured brigade, i.e., roughly 60,000 personnel. Such augmentation also involves purchase of weapon systems to equip the new troops, so we will have yet another case of scarce resources being diverted for a wasteful purpose.

The turnout at recruitment rallies is huge, especially because government jobs are considered attractive. This also makes for skewed development since the jobs are primarily meant for adult males. To put it in another way, it is for want of any other alternative that a job in the Armed Forces of the Union becomes appealing. But whatever gloss is placed on these jobs, it cannot be denied that such employment generation meant to enhance the military's suppressive role is neither socially useful nor an effective way to utilize human resources.

The factor of motivation is an important component to enable anyone to function effectively. Sebastian Junger writing about US troops in Afghanistan points out that 'it's hard to aim a rifle when your heart is pounding, which points to an irony of modern combat: it does extraordinarily violent things to the human body but requires almost dead calm to execute well'. He says that

> motor skills start to diminish at 145 beats per minute, which wouldn't matter much in a sword-fight but could definitely ruin your aim with a rifle. At 170 beats per minute you start to experience tunnel vision, loss of depth perception, and restricted hearing. And at 180 beats per minute you enter a netherworld where rational thought decays, bowel and bladder control are lost, and you start to exhibit the crudest sort of survival behaviours: freezing, fleeing, and submission.[35]

It is only motivation that can overcome the normal human response to a 'do or die' situation.

Regularly, the Armed Forces of the Union (AFU) make demands for higher salaries and benefits. One cannot blame the soldiers for demanding more and better facilities because, if they are not ideologically convinced, and are in the Armed Forces of the Union for want of better alternatives they have to draw inspiration from somewhere else. Seeking more money and perks and better 'working' conditions or regular peacetime postings as compensation for the time served in war zones is not an unfair demand. It's obvious that all those who work for wages tend to demand more. Then there is the demand that every personnel, even those fighting their own people, should be considered a 'shahid' (martyr) and receive the same benefits as the army personnel get when they are either disabled or die in the line of duty. This has been conceded and for the first time in sixty-six years, a jawan or an officer who dies fighting his own people will be considered a 'martyr'. That a soldier or an officer of the Indian military – suppressing a people who are either calling for something eminently democratic and peaceful such as the right of self-determination or a people fighting for their land, forest and livelihood against a capricious establishment determined to enable foreign and domestic mineral conglomerates – access to exploit the buried weal–this accorded a status of a 'martyr' tells its own story of the iniquitous system and how those fighting for their self-preservation get reduced to the status of 'non-persons'.

It is not as though the soldiers fighting war at home get nothing. But clamour for more never ceases. Thus a National Security Guard commander, which is an AFU administered by the Ministry of Home Affairs, receives at retirement a gratuity of Rs 2,11,450; commutation of a pension of Rs 11,35,809; Armed Forces Provident Fund of Rs 6,48,195; Army Group Insurance of Rs 1,13,849; Army Group Disability Cover of Rs 10 lakh, and, is also entitled to Rs 9 lakh for 100 per cent disability, as well as a sanctioned pension of Rs 25,254 per month.[36] Moreover, soldiers in other AFUs receive all this in addition to getting allowances as compensation for them being deployed in inhospitable battle zones.

Recently, when the Union government announced a rethink on LPG and reduced the number of cylinders for each family to six, the AFU protested and demanded that they be treated on a par with army soldiers and continue to get subsidized LPG. Their argument was that 'we are also fighting a war'.[37]

The point is that the armed forces personnel join the services for wages, and a better compensation package is a recurrent demand. While the simulated concern over the plight of the 'soldier' helps him in getting his demands fulfilled, if a similar demand was raised by any other section of the population, they would be damned and castigated for being irresponsible. Thus, para teachers getting Rs 3000 per month for years in most parts of India dare not raise their voice lest they suffer not only lathi blows but lose their jobs. In contrast, when soldiers make a demand, the government has to accommodate it. Not a whimper will be heard against this. And there is no end to security personnel's 'woes' – they routinely complain about the quality of food and shelter provided to them. There is also the constant refrain that these soldiers fighting wars on behalf of the 'nation' are being short-changed and/or getting demoralized, which is a way of exacting more resources from the exchequer. So what is it that motivates such soldiers? Is it the lure of the job and the compensation package, or is it about selfless service to the nation?

This is in marked contrast to the Maoist guerrilla.

A pamphlet which is part of a Maoist recruitment drive (from 2 December 2009 to 10 February 2010) for its PLGA (People's Liberation Guerrilla Army), carries an appeal to unemployed boys and girls of Bastar not to join the government's armed forces. The leaflet says that upon joining PLGA,

> you will not get any salary but food, clothes, personal needs will be fulfilled and your families would be helped by the Janatam Sarkar. What you will earn will be love and affection of the people. Whereas those who join government armed forces will get salary and right to loot, kill and rape but also earn undying hatred of the people and you will not be remembered. Instead your death will be celebrated.

Another leaflet tells the personnel of the government armed forces that their war is akin to the wars waged by foreign aggressors against our own people. Towards the end, the leaflet is addressed to those joining the government armed forces:

> Government does not regard you as anything more than animals. Indeed, no better than slaves. Sometimes you are called dogs (Greyhound), sometimes snakes (Cobra) and sometimes cats (Black Cats).

The flipside of 'love and affection' finds its way in another pamphlet brought out by the Dandakaranya (DK) Special Zonal Committee for a three-day bandh (25–27 January 2010), which contained an appeal to the police and paramilitary forces inviting them to ponder over why the government had launched Operation Greenhunt. The pamphlet – after reminding them that they are fighting a war in the interest of the capitalists and foreign multinationals and that they are being asked 'to kill and get reward, or get killed and receive compensation' – also reminds them of their class roots; then it appeals to them to cease using their weapons against their own class brethrens, which would earn them the people's hatred.

There is substantiation for this. In an interview with Supriya Sharma for the *Times of India*, an unnamed SPO says:

> If you work for the Naxals you don't get any money. Once a year a pant and a gamcha [towel]. If it tears you have to stitch it and wear it again. People here want to work, build homes, buy cars. But where will they earn the money from. I had a tractor but no money for fuel. On top of it, the Naxals said do not sell paddy. Give it to the poor. Is that fair? The poor of course were happy with them [the Maoists]. The poor are their biggest support base . . . First I trained with the Nagas [CRPF Naga Bn]. Then I was sent to train with the Army in Kashmir. But I tell you, the training was nothing in comparison with the training given by Naxals. They have a lot of 'jazba' [enthusiasm] . . . [police] still do not fully trust us [adivasis].[38]

The difference between a guerrilla and a professional soldier could not have been better described.

A copy of the public apology circulated by the DK Special Zonal Committee on 28 April 2009, addressed to the family of those killed in a landmine explosion on 16 April 2009, makes for interesting reading. The poster-pamphlet provided a complete explanation. It said:

> We know by saying sorry your dear departed will not return nor our apology wipe out your tears. But we wish to tell you that our Party had no animosity with your dear ones. It was an accident. Government servants including policemen and ordinary police personnel posted with paramilitary formations are not our enemy . . . You can then ask us why do we attack police and paramilitary forces? Why do we put landmines? Or why do we have to use 'violence'? In reality the system is responsible for this . . . You know very well that every peaceful agitation and struggle faces lathi-charge and bullets. We are neither extremists nor terrorists as is being

> propagated by this government of exploiting classes. We are children of workers, peasants and middle classes . . . We are organizing people in the backward tribal areas against their exploitation and oppression so that they can fight for their rights.

The difference between two forms of soldiering thus gets revealed.[39]

The pamphlet describes what happened in and around Singaram in south Bastar on 4 January 2009 where nineteen adivasis were killed, four of them women. The women were gangraped and then killed. Around the same time in west Bastar's Minkapalli, six adivasis were killed. Since 2005, at least 1000 Adivasis have been killed, hundreds of women raped, and 700 villages burnt, says the pamphlet:

> All this is being done to hand over mineral wealth of DK forests to multinationals and foreign capitalists. It is against this violence we have been compelled to answer with 'violence'. Had we not resisted they would have succeeded in their objective. Of course jawans in police and paramilitary forces belong to ordinary peasant and worker families or middle-class families but they have become tools in the hands of exploiters and are attacking those amongst whom they grew up. Killing, looting, raping, making illegal arrests, taking bribes . . . this is the common practice of the police force . . . Many a time we have distributed pamphlets appealing to them not to attack poor and exploited people. This is the context in which we use landmines and attack police and armed forces.

In other words, the motivation of a professional soldier and a revolutionary is vastly different. Both may fight heroically, bravely, but the one who is fighting without wages and is self-motivated is vastly different and far superior to one fighting for wages and on whom discipline has to be imposed. The possibility of commission of crime by a government force is also far higher because they aim to force people to snap links with the rebels, whereas for the guerrillas without the people's support their very survival is at stake. An anonymous soldier explained to *Tehelka* magazine:

> I always wanted to be a sainik [soldier] to serve my country, but now I feel I will be dying for nothing. I have seen so many illegal things happening. We have to blindly follow orders. When we go for operations, we don't know who a Maoist is. Poor Adivasis are being beaten and innocents are being killed. I don't feel that I am doing anything for the nation. My patriotism is dead.[40]

This inability to either recognize motivation or fully grasp the many dimensions of military suppression and an intellectual's contribution towards honing the skills meant to suppress and then pacify a recalcitrant population is captured well by India's most celebrated psychoanalyst Sudhit Kakar:

> The role of a community's women in its men taking up arms, or in the making of a terrorist, has not been appreciated enough. Whether it was Punjab in the late 1980s, or Kashmir in the last two decades or even other places around the world, there is no stronger goad to arousing a man's fighting spirit than that of a woman mocking and challenging his masculinity. Militancy starts losing its vigour once the women turn away from demanding masculinity from their men and begin to think more of survival and well-being of their children. Unfortunately, anti-terror efforts are rarely directed towards influencing a community's women.[41]

The author need not worry about the number of studies and research focusing on women, precisely as an extension of counter-insurgency pacification is being undertaken by singling out women and essentializing their experience whereas the entire society was affected, some more, others less, but no one remained unscathed. So intellectuals come in handy to provide additional means to the military suppression by advocating targeting of women, completely ignoring how soldiers target women and use their vulnerability for sexual exploitation. But even erudite scholars sometimes gloss over other aspects of reality.

The proposition above would work in, say, Punjab or Kashmir where women act as motivators or assist in ways other than directly engaging in combat. But in revolutionary warfare this divide falls flat. CPI (Maoists) have 45-60 per cent women guerrillas. In such a situation using the argument of community and its women goading/motivating men to pick up arms and fight does not work. Here, men as well as women participate, each motivating the other. All work is shared. Here, such tricks as trying to single out women, and the entire scholarship that places women as intrinsically attuned to peace, etc., stands exposed as being a lot of hot air.

What is the point? Simply that revolutionary warfare has specificity and ground-breaking capability to overcome and/or break divides which a class-caste society considers 'natural'.

Thus the context and the objective put the two forms of soldiering, so to say, in different orbits.

How does one then explain the selfless work during natural calamities and disasters where the very same professional jawans render yeomen's service? The difference lies in the distinction between war and disaster rescue and relief operations. It's not as though soldiers are inherently predatory or inherently heroic because of the nature of their profession. It is the nature of war that they are deputed to fight, particularly against our own people designated 'enemy' by the commanders and decision-makers, which defines their soldiering in internal wars. In such situations, a commanding officer plays a catalytic role. He/she can ensure that soldiers act with restraint and do not rape, molest, torture, loot or engage in blood-letting. Alternately, the same commanding officer can use his/her authority in encouraging them to go berserk. On top of that, even when a commander encourages a soldier to 'do whatever', the soldier or officer cannot escape the choice he/she has of not raping, torturing or killing those in custody or killing anyone under the fallacious argument of doing so 'in the heat of the moment'. Natural disasters are moments that help bring out their inherent ability to rise above themselves and offer selfless service as a collective, disciplined effort. To read either one or the other as the defining characteristic of soldiering would be misplaced, especially in India, because of the propensity of the Indian State to wage wars against our own people. In other words, it is the circumstance and the context that defines a soldier's role.

# 5
# Monopoly over Violence

In the light of all this, many insist that non-violence is the only way out. While we may prefer non-violent methods, unfortunately the choice is never really in the hands of the people. Neither does the fate of non-violent movements inspire confidence about their longevity or about their capacity to counter the State, nor is it certain that a peaceful seizure of power is at all possible. The much-vaunted non-violence of the Indian National Congress (INC) did not lessen the violent military suppression carried out by the British Raj. It can be argued that the Indian National Congress derived its advantage and became a preferred partner for dialogue with the British Raj because of the presence of armed or violent struggles. Moreover, the INC's use of violence against its political opponents or the practice of communal politics when it first came to power in 1935 leaves the votaries of non-violence with uncomfortable questions which they generally skirt. In any case, there is a strong case in favour of asserting that people's reason for picking up arms rests on whether a peaceful democratic political resolution is possible or not. People do not have the propensity to get violent unless they are driven to it and it becomes a matter of self-preservation. Take Kashmir, for instance. For two decades, India's 'good' people propagated to Kashmiris to give up their armed militancy and said that this could bring about a sea change in the Indian people's capacity to consider even the most radical demands of the 'azadi' movement. Later, for three years, mass protests replaced armed militancy. When the 'good' people suddenly discovered that militancy has ended and the movement has fizzled out, they decided that there was no need for more than minor tinkering to fix things in Kashmir. Now, once again, with Afzal Guru's hanging, and the strangulation of Kashmiris to ensure that protests do not ensue, the message that is going out to the Kashmiris is that they will only be heard and taken seriously when there is militancy; or else, the monopoly enjoyed over the means of violence by the Indian State will prevail to suppress their democratic aspirations.

In the essay 'Politics and Violence', Uday S. Mehta writes:

> Non-violence for Gandhi is not a cognate of peace. It does not refer, as it does in the tradition of political thinking, to a condition of public order secured through the surrounding proximity of fear, punishment and power . . . [For Gandhi] peace, war and politics is indifferent to the issue of violence . . . the three terms are neither fundamentally disposed to violence, nor are they, more importantly, fundamentally opposed to violence. The relationship between peace, war and violence is strictly conditional. The normative status of each of these terms depends on a political calculation in which the 'security' of the political community (the state) plays a decisive role. It is an implication of this claim that there is no principled, and hence strong, commitment to non-violence or an opposition to war; nor is there a fundamental orientation to abjuring from the use of physical force in the modern conception of peace.[42]

He points out:

> Weber's definition of the state as having a monopoly on the legitimate use of violence is largely just a more blunt restatement of the more general claim that if public interest must be an over-riding priority, then the state must have the means to assert that priority. Violence cannot, given this priority, be proscribed in principle.[43] . . . [V]iolence can be an instrument for peace and order and that order itself has no clear relationship with violence or its opposite . . . Alternatively violence may be something that undermines order. Precisely because it can go both ways politics can take no principled view on the matter of violence . . .[44] [M]ost modern wars have been authorized in the name of peace and order. In India, we are of course witness to a savage war, in the shape of Operation Greenhunt being carried out in the name of development.

Thus when John Keegan argues for 'warriors for civilisation', there are underlying assumptions that need to be interrogated. Wars for profit or advantage can masquerade as wars for Peace, Development, and restoring Law and Order. Thus, such keywords attempt to distinguish one combatant from the other, glorifying one and demonizing the other. This is most acutely felt in internal wars where rebel combatants are criminalized and robbed of their history, and even their motivations and the context.

It has also become abundantly clear that nation-states have a powerful weapon in the shape of proscription of organizations and criminalization of every activity otherwise considered legitimate for political associations. The Coordination of Democratic Rights Organisation in its report *The Terror of Law: UAPA and the Myth of National Security* (Delhi 2012) on the Unlawful Activities (Prevention) Act 1967, points out how member states of the UN have subverted the norm of regulating and containing war by virtually practising an absolute form of war in which the opposite side is to sought to be demonized for eventual annihilation.[45] This is done by rendering an 'irregular' or 'partisan' into someone 'illegal' or nothing more than criminal, while simultaneously immunizing their own armed personnel by ensuring that their forces do not get hauled up for war crimes or they are exempted from being covered by laws that govern wars, such as the Geneva Conventions and Protocols. The report says:

> If the definition of terror acts had been proximate to war crimes, i.e. terrorist acts are war crimes committed in peace time, then the crime itself gets outlawed through punitive measures against all those who carry out such criminal acts. But if certain 'entities' get proscribed as though they are the only ones committing crimes against Humanity then it is not the crime itself but some select 'entities' who are held responsible for such acts and they get persecuted. Exclusion of agencies of State is inevitable because the UN SC is foremost a political decision-maker, neither a legislative body nor a juridical body applying legal principles. It's a body made up of member nation-states. Thus it follows that its lack of definition or use of discrete understanding of what constitutes 'terrorist acts' allows every member state to specify whom they consider illegitimate or proscribe.

Here, two things are worth noting that war crimes define illegal conduct during wars or armed conflicts and place the onus on both adversaries not to harm civilians, be they forces of two States or as in civil war between the State and rebels, or the irregulars of international concern. The UN Resolutions, adopted since 2001, have illegalized the 'irregulars'. And by bringing 'attacks on the Government' and not just civilians into consideration, they allow the member states to illegitimize anyone who challenge their authority or rebel against them within their own borders. Thus, the politics that is integral to understanding the growth of armed conflict within nation-state borders gets muted. For instance, the partition of India and the division of Jammu and Kashmir in 1947 and the consequent history cannot be separated from the movement for 'azadi' because without that, the brutal history of the past twenty-two years loses its political poignancy. Anyhow, it has enabled the government to regard militants fighting for self-determination or people wanting to resist takeover of their land, forest and water, as being no different from those who carry out deliberate killings of civilians in the name of religion, race or nationalism.

In other words, the fact that member states of the UN are at liberty to proscribe anyone or turn rebellion into a crime does not mean that law is all-deciding. It only brings out how rebels are placed at a disadvantage by the member states, until they manage to compel recognition from the people and a reluctant government. The Indian government's record throws up this factor again and again. Blowing hot and cold, banning and criminalizing rebels have not come in the way of according recognition to and negotiating with rebels at times. So what matters is how rebels are perceived by the people and whether they enjoy legitimacy in their eyes and, last but not the least, if it appears that they cannot be crushed militarily.

It is also important to note that when the State wages war against its own people, it is accompanied by legal authorization which allows it to criminalize dissent per se by cracking down on anyone as an 'overground worker'. But what is not realized is that the Intelligence Bureau is tasked with carrying out de-radicalization. What this means is that the corporate media, publishers, universities and colleges, all ensure that literature considered 'radical' or a person labelled 'radical' are prevented from gaining acceptability. So their books, films, plays, music and songs shall not find a place in the public space; nor will their statements be carried by the media. Just compare the ease with which mass murderers, rapists, and looters of public funds have easy access to the media, whereas those espousing radical thoughts without even committing crimes get barred, censored and/or marginalized. Compare how scurrilous writings find their way out but writings that expose the predatory nature of the State are suppressed. This is the flip side of war, of what takes place outside the war zones, but is part of the same.

It is also worth noting that countries like India (US, China, Russia, etc.) manage to escape from any accountability for their military actions and war crimes because quite apart from a lack of will, domestic laws do not even criminalize acts like torture, enforced disappearance and genocide. When the UN undertook its periodic universal review of human rights in India in April 2012, the Indian government simply rejected all the recommendations that asked India to bring its domestic laws in line with international laws, conventions and protocols, and claimed that there were no armed conflicts in the country. In other words, in the twenty-first century, countries such as India can evade responsibility and allow war crimes to go unpunished without any fear or concern by simply denying these internal wars and retaining a legal system that protects government troops from fear of prosecution.

In this sense, in our own times the prospects of war being regulated and contained gets blunted because by criminalizing one side of the combatants, the government can wipe them out as one would presumably wipe out crooks and criminals. Yet, it would be misplaced to exaggerate this, because the rebels have managed to get around this debilitation built into nation-states and its so-called rule of law by retaining the all-important popular support, forcing the government to accord them respect. Thus in India, the government blows hot and cold depending upon whether it believes the rebels are weak or strong.

In this connection, the third preamble to the Declaration of Human Rights, 1948, is interesting where it says that

> [w]hereas it is essential, if man is not to be compelled to have recourse, as a last resort, to rebellion against tyranny and oppression, that human rights should be protected by the rule of law.

In other words, rebellion is an inherent and inalienable right when the State, which enjoys a monopoly over the means of violence, employs it, for example, to defend the present status quo, while reproducing oppressive social relations. Such conditions, real or potential, enable the ruling classes to subject many to a life of indignity and enslavement wherein freedom and liberty remain the prerogative of the upper and middle classes. So, a worker, Dalit or Adivasi, or a youth found with Marxist literature or even B.R. Ambedkar's works or the legendary Bhagat Singh's books, is often seen as a real or potential Naxalite, just as an educated Muslim youth, expressing his views about injustice against those who happen to be Muslims, is perceived as a real or potential 'jehadi'. Under these circumstances, the working class is particularly vulnerable: no sooner do they appear to have succeeded in mobilizing a union, questioning the inequalities and inadequacies of the system, than they become target of the State's oppressive ways. Therefore, unless the State is made to outlaw war against its own people, i.e., till it disengages from a *prolonged violent suppression of those people* fighting for a life of dignity and for the right to determine their future, one cannot neutralize the great advantage the ruling classes enjoy over the means of violence, primarily employed against the exploited and the oppressed.

Therefore, when discussing the rights and wrongs of war/violence, '[s]ound ethics requires us to always to judge the action by the results, good or bad, and not by its conformity to a rule, regardless of results'.[46] It is argued that

> [t]he principle that it is never right to depart from moral principles, even to achieve some good end, no matter how many people would suffer if the rule were not broken, far from reflecting a superior ethical standpoint, is supremely unethical and is generally regarded as such. And thus, the 'real issue . . . over means and ends is not therefore as to whether we may or may not adopt means involving evil to attain a good which outbalances that evil or to avoid a still greater evil, but as to whether the good attained is really worth the cost, or whether there is another route to that good involving less evil'.[47]

India is one of the most heavily armed states both in terms of the accumulation of destructive weapons into its arsenal as also in terms of the size of its military, which gets force multiplied by draconian laws, thus enabling the ruling classes to also get away with 'slow genocide'.[48] To belittle this dismal reality by arguing that this is structural violence, a product of policies or has to do with systemic faults, and is not caused by use of direct physical violence, and so, it is less important than political violence, means it is an ideological construct to downplay the complicity of the rulers in causing the slow death of millions or subjecting them to gross inequalities, due to the policies or the lack of them.

In such conditions, armed resistance plays an emancipatory role, as the oppressed are able to defend themselves, save themselves from being trampled upon by a ruthless military which invariably sides with the powerful and the privileged. This is accepted even by as officious an organization as the Indian Planning Commission in its report *Development Challenges in Extremist Affected Area* prepared by an expert group.[49] Thus to pick up guns, to learn to handle guns, to harness them for the greater common good cannot per se be considered 'evil' because violence is value neutral. It is how violence is harnessed and for what purpose it is used that are of relevance. To assume that just because right-wing extremists use violence and therefore there is no difference between how they use it and how anyone else uses it is a gross misrepresentation of social reality. To argue that death caused by a fascist or a Maoist is one and the same because the fact is that a person has died, is an argument fraught with contradiction. By this logic, the deaths of rioters at the hands of security forces are on a par with those of people killed in fake encounters (euphemism for custodial killing or extra-judicial execution) carried out by the security forces. Or, the lynching to death by the slum dwellers of Nagpur of a rapist and extortionist gangster is the same as the caste panchayat issuing a diktat to kill those who fall in love outside their caste or lineage! This makes inconsequential the difference between radical right-wing groups for whom a community/race is the enemy and terrorizing civilians is considered legitimate, and the violence of the left-wing radicals whose focus is on ending the material conditions of oppression of the people.

Those who decry armed struggle claim that peaceful movements can make existing institutions of the State responsive to people's needs. However, such efforts were being made even when the Maoists had not emerged as the single biggest threat to the Indian ruling classes, and these efforts have not ceased because of the Maoist rebellion. It is estimated that 50,000 people die every day in 'poverty related deaths', preventable through better nutrition, safe drinking water, vaccines and medicines. How come it is only now, when the Maoists have entered the picture that these issues have begun to prick the conscience of India's ruling class, even if hypocritically? In this sense, it would be worth exploring how many tens of millions of lives have been saved thanks to the Maoist resistance. It is doubtful whether, without the threat of the Maoists, the ruling classes would have shown much interest in pushing for reducing poverty in the age of neo-liberalism, which is grounded on subsidizing the rich and cutting down on subsidy that benefits the underprivileged. Moreover, non-violent struggles actually gained some elbow room because of the presence and strengthening of the Maoist Movement; they have been leveraging the armed struggle of the Maoists to extract concessions/reforms from the State. It is doubtful if they would have counted for much had it not been for the Maoist armed struggle.

In order to make things conceptually clear, I want to make another point. There are some who point to certain actions of the Maoists (mutilation of dead bodies, beheading, people's court awarding death sentences, killing of 'informers', attack on economic 'assets'), and from that arrive at the conclusion that these acts carry within them 'social impact', and insist that no achievement lasts if it is brought about violently. There are others who go a step further and argue that whether or not the Maoists commit crimes, the very fact that they are armed and justify violence suffices to raise questions about the strategy and tactics of a movement, its understanding of social reality, and mars the chances of a State and society, where weapons in possession of one party can be used to cow down people in general and political opponents in particular.

There is nothing mechanical in this at all. Despite the revolutionary transformation of China brought about through war and the relatively peaceful transfer of power in India, it did not make China more violent than India. And were structural violence to be foregrounded, India would rank much higher than China precisely because all social indices show that people in China are better off than in India. At the same time, India and China are equally illiberal in their constriction of freedom in myriad ways. Moreover, for all the claims of free media in India, their right-wing and more loyal-than-the-king perspective makes the Indian corporate media occupy a position of hostility where fundamental issues of oppression and exploitation are concerned. Little wonder then that India holds rank 134 in the human development index and 140 in the world media review survey of media freedom.

The question is what should be done to reduce the possibility of a dictatorship that could emerge using the fig leaf of being a 'vanguard', patriot, etc. What matters also is the politics of those spearheading war and how open they are to criticism and to changing their ways when confronted with fault lines.

In the 1990s, Maoists in DK heeded the criticism that the people's courts were awarding death sentences all too often. This was then corrected and the incidence of death sentences declined. They have also shown a willingness to allow the removal of the injured and the dead by even letting helicopters enter into their area. The treatment of prisoners too has been exemplary. So there is reason not to hype their war crimes. But what about their commitment to dissent, criticism and to the democratic freedoms of the people? Will they live up to respecting divergence and difference were they to come to power?

These apprehensions about armed struggle and victors silencing those they dislike or crushing dissent tend to lend credibility to efforts designed to push the war towards the Clausewitzian notion of 'real war', i.e., a war which is regulated and then brought to an end with a negotiated solution. Because either one side will vanquish the other and impose its will or there will be a negotiated settlement in which case an orderly solution can take place. In the present context of Maoists versus the State, with military victory for any one side a distant possibility, the containment of war appears a realistic option, *even if we are at present far removed from that possibility*. That's because the State is cocky that it can wipe out the Maoists, whereas the Maoists show that they are resilient to such prospect.

It is argued by some that any organized military force is in itself anti-democratic, whereas violence that ensues as a result of mass uprising is all right. Contrarily, it should be pointed out that a spontaneous recourse to violence can cause greater harm. In France after the Second World War, more than 40,000 people were lynched for being 'collaborators' of the Nazi occupation force. Would we justify this lynching in the name of spontaneous reaction of the people freed from Nazi tyranny? In fact, it is in the nature of violence, as with fire, that it must be harnessed or else it can cause greater damage than good. Therefore, what is regarded as anti-democratic, i.e., training, hierarchy and discipline, are of utmost necessity. Fascist political formations use the spontaneous mass-violence path to gloss over their deliberate targeting of minorities or Left and progressive elements. It is when force is harnessed and guerrillas are self-motivated that rebels become open to understanding the ethics of war. They are ready to take action against anyone in their rank who violates those rules. A ragtag band is incapable of adhering to this discipline and tends to be less accountable.

Arguably, this means that my opposition to the State's recourse to military suppression must be tempered by this reasoning. But I believe that when armed forces are sent to suppress a people it is part of their brief to terrorize the civilians. They are expected to suppress the people precisely in order to crush the insurgency. Of course, one must also be clear that soldiers are rarely prosecuted for homicide, because that is part of their job profile—the nature of their training is to 'kill or get killed'. But even these soldiers should not escape prosecution, for rape, torture, looting, etc. What is more important, the insurgents cannot afford to violate the ethics of war, i.e., they should neither be brutal nor cruel, or else they will lose their biggest advantage—voluntary mass support. A people's support for the revolutionaries based on fear is not designed to last.

Let's take two counter-arguments. One is that those committed to non-violence ought to stand up against all wars waged by the Indian State. If they do not, then their intellectual commitment to non-violence is subject to doubt. Secondly, independent of what is done or not done by those against violence of all types, other processes influence the course of an armed resistance. In Kashmir, commentators jumped to the conclusion that people got tired of militant violence and opted for a peaceful way, getting on with their lives and elections. But the fatigue with militancy does not explain a few anomalies. Why do funeral processions of militants continue to attract a large number of people? Why does such a huge deployment of troops remain in the state, controlling the private and public lives of people if they (people) were so fed up with 'separatists' and militants? Why is holding a protest or staging a rally prohibited for Kashmiris, while the military is engaged in 'draining' people of 'wrong' ideas such as 'azadi'? The dynamics of people-militants relationship reveals the role played by militancy in not just keeping the spirit of defiance alive but also in providing people self-confidence and courage. Stone pelters or the mass upsurge of 2008 were not a disavowal of armed resistance but an acknowledgement that militancy without mass struggle will not work. It is the Kashmiris' own lived experience which propelled the movement into this direction.

Having said this, let us move beyond. There is violence and violence. Therefore, a distinction must be drawn between spectacular raids such as for looting armouries, freeing prisoners and defending what is called 'janta sarkar' as in Bastar, and heinous acts such as beheading or custodial killing. But not all crimes attributed to Maoists/Naxalites have been committed by them. In the 2008 Nayagarh (Orissa) incident, the media carried unsubstantiated reports of Maoists mutilating the bodies of dead soldiers. Some eminent persons issued a statement without even bothering to verify the facts of the matter. Then the Khagaria massacre in September 2009 was attributed to the Maoists, although it later turned out to be a caste conflict over forty bighas of land. Thus, the Jehanabad jail break, for example, was criticized by the 'good' people of India on the grounds that it would provoke possible retaliation by the landlord armies in Bihar upon the poor. This did not happen. But it did expose the administration as being capable of stopping the landlord armies if it so wishes. This enhanced rather than eroded the sense of security of the landless Dalit agricultural labour. The fighting skills of the Maoist guerrillas too need to be taken into account as evident in the battle of 20 August 2011 at Makadchuha village in Gadchiroli district of Maharashtra.

Thirty Maoist guerrillas led by a woman commander Raneeta, also known as Ramko Hichami, held off 250 commandos, which included CRPF's COBRA units, for ten hours while all that the Maoist guerrillas were carrying were .303 rifles.

This is not to say that the Maoists have been upright in all circumstances and above criticism or fault. When civilians are attacked, when Maoist cadres target passenger trains, and when they repeat their mistakes, questions are raised about the so-called People's War. However, the critics should know that the Maoists have been rather forthright in accepting criticism as well as in engaging in debate. In fact, no other Naxal group has ever engaged in debate with so many groups and individuals over the past forty years as the Maoists and their forerunner PU and PWG. While the role of the Committee of Concerned Citizens in Andhra Pradesh has been acknowledged, we cannot ignore the fact that *the CCC's contribution lay in drawing out CPIML (PW), into a dialogue with them which was a valuable exchange and it could materialize because the Maoists showed willingness to engage in this.* Why just that; they were second to none in responding to the CCC's entreaties to come for negotiations. In other words, if the CCC is credited with drawing them into a dialogue, the CPI ML (PW) deserves to be credited with fusing life into the effort and never flinching from responding to the initiatives of the democratic-minded intelligentsia.

Conventional wisdom says that wars are dirty and, no matter what, they will be brutish because of the very nature of the engagement. This appears to be an attractive proposition for those who hide behind such explanations to fulminate against wars as such. It is a myth that soldiers simply go berserk in certain situations. As a matter of fact, it is possible for an army to desist from committing atrocities.

A commander can stop his soldiers from being brutish and, equally, also permit them to terrorize people. It is not an aberration or a momentary lapse that causes atrocities. It is a deliberate decision of the field commander that turns disciplined soldiers into predators. Even in the heat of the battle, it is possible for a commander to ensure that soldiers under his/her command neither disobey nor commit crimes. If invariably government soldiers fail to maintain this discipline, it is because the counter-insurgency doctrine is based on 'draining the water' so the 'fish' do not survive. It is the nature of the warfare that the government forces fight which allows for the commission of crimes. In contrast, for the insurgents, retaining the support of the people is a matter of life or death. For all the arguments of 'pent up fury of the oppressed', a guerrilla is far less indisciplined and far less brutish. The very nature of the warfare they fight makes it necessary. In both cases, a disciplined force can and does display restraint. Some insist that in a frenzy soldiers do not remember their training and just turn into killers. But those who argue thus forget that a soldier has the choice of not engaging in excessive killing, rape or torture. To believe that they cannot stop themselves in the heat of the moment and are somehow victims of their peculiar circumstances is lazy intellectualism divorced from reality. Soldiers can and do stop themselves even when their commander gives them a go-ahead to do the contrary.

But what about the killing of 'informers' and the role of the People's Court? As a DR activist, I oppose custodial killing. Years of efforts have at least made the Maoists accept that their party would consider the issues raised as well as take a position on compliance with the Geneva Conventions, especially Protocol II. And I believe we must remain engaged with them, precisely because they form an integral and leading part of India's resistance movement which would suffer irrevocably were they to be defeated. Their very presence acts as a restraint on the ruling classes not to go all out against non-violent resistance, lest this result in enhancing the appeal of armed struggle. So their direct and indirect contribution to ameliorating the conditions of people or restraining the State from indulging in all-out suppression cannot be ignored. But there is something more fundamental at stake.

As DR activists, we also recognize the Maoists are carrying on a legitimate political movement, one criminalized and delegitimized by the politics of ban through the aegis of laws such as the UAPA. On one hand, the government denies fighting a war (passing it off as 'police action') but at the same time every Maoist party member is accused of 'waging war' and/or sedition. What does this imply? It means that by terming them as criminals or terrorists or anarchists, the State and its acolytes rob them of their context, history and legitimacy. In contrast, war obliges us to accord legitimacy to both sides, to not only restore humanity to those demonized but to fight for acknowledging them as a political movement. To argue that there is no war may be second nature to 'sarkari' intellectuals, but those who accept that there is a war/armed conflict must understand that neither the Indian Constitution nor the Indian Penal Code are capable of or have shown any capacity to protect people from the government forces' voracious appetite for atrocities. If the Army Act or the CPMF Acts define that every armed personnel posted in a conflict zone is on 'active duty' or 'active service' twenty-four hours a day, the Supreme Court simultaneously advances the ludicrous proposition that it would be presumed that armed personnel act in 'good faith' and that this presumption cannot be 'dislodged' even when there is prima facie evidence of commission of a crime by an armed personnel belonging to the government against a civilian/non-combatant. Why? Because the Court cannot take cognition of the evidence unless there is government sanction for it to do so. So we have a situation where two laws operate. One for the unarmed civilians and another for government combatants. So even if rape, torture or killings occur and the victims are civilians, the extant law ordains that it would be presumed that the government soldier acted in 'good faith'. Furthermore, it is for AFUs to decide whether they would try their personnel or refer it to a civilian court.

Under such circumstances, to essentialize the issue of Maoist violence or to make ill-informed generalizations about war being this and that and senseless violence as being intrinsic might appear an attractive stance but this is the way in which a class society dehumanizes struggles and movements. Besides, there are as many instances of movements degenerating because they use violence as there are of those which use non-violent methods. But the bottom line is that the reproduction of social inequality is unacceptable. Those who believe in a step-by-step process, and those who swear by a leap or a qualitative jump from one stage to another must accept that there will remain a divide, and both must respect each other. Those who decry armed struggle claim that peaceful movements can make existing institutions responsive to people's needs. The point is that these movements get crushed, co-opted and contained before they ever reach a stage where they can challenge authority. In any case, these efforts have not ceased because of the Maoist rebellion; rather, I would argue that these movements have actually gained some space, and are using the Maoist presence to espouse their politics, which would probably have been ignored otherwise.

The rout of NDA government in 2004 was directly related to its pursuit and promotion of predatory global capitalism.

The experience of the *silenced* majority under UPA rule I and II has been of big words and small deeds. The biggest deal for the 'aam aadmi' was the NREGA (National Rural Employment Guarantee Act). But was it not the fear of Maoists that ensured the passage of NREGA and the formulation of the forest bill? Why only that; isn't the recent decision of the Jharkhand administration to withdraw cases filed against at least one lakh Adivasis – so as to wean them away from the Maoists – not something where credit must again go to the rebels? Thus, Maoists have their use too for reformers who leverage them for pushing reforms.

Besides, consider what the Home Minister told the Lok Sabha on 7 July 2009:

> [N]axalism is no longer a disjointed or uncoordinated actions by groups in states. Today naxalism is directed by CPI (Maoist) which is now a very structured organization. It even has a Central Military Command.

In other words, they are now a strong, organized military force capable of launching multiple simultaneous attacks, in which several groups of 200–500 armed cadres travel long distances, escaping a network of surveillance/ intelligence/informers. Equally important to note is that without people identifying themselves with the Maoists, voluntarily and not out of fear, this fairly large social support base cannot be sustained.

Now the Indian State propagates that the Naxalites are irredeemably bent upon waging a war against the State and are anti-development. Thus, short of suppressing them there is no other option. Of course, Maoists want to seize power. Certainly those who take up arms cannot escape opprobrium for violations of principles, in what they themselves regard as People's War. But this is the more important question: what brought this about? It did not happen overnight but over nearly five decades. In this period, several groups gave up armed struggle to pursue non-violent, parliamentary or extra-parliamentary struggle. Their experience hardly inspires confidence that the Indian State has become amenable to people's concerns. In this sense, appeal, if not the prospect of non-violence, has been undermined by the state itself. What is so remarkable about this? How does it make non-violent political transformation attractive? If struggle for power requires positioning for strength, why should Maoists try what has failed *(the peaceful way)*, and not do *what is necessary (offer armed resistance)*?

However, precisely because violence is *value neutral*, it is human beings who invest it with ethical values and meanings. Therefore, armed struggle impacts political developments. Unlike a war between two states, where regular forces fight each other, in a civil war-like situation the warring sides are not so clearly profiled. If the official doctrine on Low Intensity Conflicts finds it seminal the 'distinction between fighting the 'enemy' and 'fighting one's own people' and there is a blurring of distinction between 'front and rear; strategic and tactical; combatants and non-combatants' as well as there 'is a need to change a soldier's mindset from fighting the 'enemy' in a conventional conflict, for which he is trained, to fighting his 'own people', then this problem afflicts the rebels too.[50] Because it is from among, say, the Adivasis themselves that their opponents also get recruited. How Maoists navigate themselves through these real or potential divisions among the people belonging to different tribe/clan/caste/ sub-caste with class differentiations often muted, and ensure that their actions do not create divisions or community of aggrieved people – rather they are able to bridge these divisions – is the challenge posed to the Maoists. In other words, the legitimacy of the armed struggle is not an issue; rather how they conduct their armed struggle and the values this revolutionary movement invests in it are of vital importance because these affect the political conduct and outcome. However, the conduct of war cannot be de-linked from how, in this case, the forces of State fight the war.

# 6

# Counter-Insurgency Doctrine

The Indian Army's Doctrine for Sub Conventional Operations in its seventy-seven pages encompasses 'collective wisdom and philosophy on fighting such operations, and also endeavours to highlight to civil society, the very basis for the Army's employment in such operations'. It begins by ruling out 'total war as an instrument of State policy' and speaks of 'further impetus' to sub-conventional operations as the '*predominant* form of warfare'. The distinction between fighting the 'enemy' and 'fighting one's own people' is a seminal difference. In this warfare, there is a blurring of distinction between 'Front and Rear; Strategic and Tactical; Combatants and Non-combatants'.[52] Therefore, there 'is a need to change a soldier's mindset from fighting the "enemy" in a conventional conflict, for which he is trained, to fighting his "own people" [53] The US Army's Counter-Insurgency manual, which is a variant of the same, says that 'all insurgencies, even today's highly adaptable strains (i.e., Al Qaeda) remain wars amongst the people'.[54, 55]

Therefore, the Indian Army doctrine says that

> the military operations should aim firstly, at neutralizing all hostile elements in the conflict zone that oppose or retard the peace initiatives and secondly, at transforming the will and attitudes of the people . . . The endeavour should be to bring

> about a realization that fighting the government is a 'no win' situation and that their anti-government stance will only delay the return of peace and normalcy. Therefore, distancing from the terrorists is in their own interest and the only plausible course of action. However, the manifestation of such a realization can take from a couple of years to decades as attitudes take time to form and to change.[56]

'Neutralizing hostile elements' or 'transforming the will and attitudes of the people' is quintessentially a muscular approach. It clearly implies *breaking* the will of the people through recourse to military suppression.

Unlike the Indian doctrine, the US doctrine is candid when it says that 'insurgency is . . . an organized, protracted politico-military struggle designed to weaken government control and legitimacy while increasing insurgent control'.[57] Since legitimacy involves both coercion and consent manufacturing, consent becomes critical. Obviously, coercion is the preferred means since 'attitudes' can take decades to change.

Therefore, the way in which the internal war is actually conducted becomes important. The Indian Army is coy about using terms like 'population control measures' as the US doctrine does. But the approaches are not too dissimilar. Of foremost importance is 'to isolate the conflict zone from external material assistance for optimal utilization of Army resources. It is, therefore, essential that any external support is intercepted and neutralized along the borders'.[58] In the hinterland, operations

> include patrolling, ambushes, raids, cordon and search, search and destroy, establishment of vehicle and personnel check posts, road opening, convoy protection and security of various static installations, that includes various operating bases.[59]

This leaves an impression that the Indian military operations or the wars conducted by the US are not as lethal as conventional wars, indeed in some sense they are even benign. The reason is that all the gory details about the actual conduct of operations hide between phrases and keywords, and they have to be culled out. Whatever the stated intent, the actual conduct of war targets people in general to ensure that they do not lend help to the rebels. For instance, both for sealing of the border and operations in the 'hinterland', heavy deployment of troops becomes necessary. Although each combat zone differs from another, they conform to certain characteristics. Thus, if minimum use of *lethal force* is required in such operations, it requires a correspondingly higher force deployment, thereby compensating for the loss in firepower through manpower.

The foreword to the US Counter-Insurgency document comes straight to the point and says that 'all insurgencies even today's highly adaptable strains remains "wars amongst the people"'.[60] In this war, the success of Counter-Insurgency (COIN) depends on

> the people taking charge of their own affair and consenting to the government rule. Achieving this condition requires the government to eliminate as many causes of the insurgency as feasible. This can include eliminating those extremists whose beliefs prevent them from ever reconciling with the government.[61]

In other words, it means 'population control' which 'includes determining who lives in an area and what they do. Establishment control normally begins with conducting a census and issuing identification cards.' Other measures to control the population include

> curfew; a pass system; limits on lengths of time people can travel; limits on number of visitors from

> outside the area with a requirement to register them with local security forces or civil authorities; check posts along major routes and enforce compliance with population control measures.[62]

In another place, without any sense of irony they say that 'insurgents are constrained by neither the law nor the bonds of human decency as Western nations understand them'.[63] And quite blasé at another level that 'after security has been achieved, dollars and ballots will have more important effects than bombs and bullets'; so 'money is ammunition'.[64]

An obvious difference between the Indian and the US approaches is that the US manual deals with COIN theatre as being outside the borders of US, whereas for India it is related to their operation within the constitutionally ordained borders. This may be the reason that US COIN includes air bombings, missile attacks, helicopter gunships, navy war ships, etc., whereas in India the approach is of heavy deployment of troops on the ground with 'area domination' as the purpose. Partly for this reason, US military adventures have carried high civilian casualties as in Indo-China and Iraq or Afghanistan, because killing of non-US citizens by the US military does not arouse much concern as it would otherwise. This may account for the higher casualties in Iraq between March 2003 to December 2006 of between 1,50,000–6,00,000, as against the two decades of death count of more than 70,000 in J&K. But whatever be the approach, both acknowledge that the hostile are from 'amongst the people'. Both use means brutal and benign, fair and foul, to bring about the people's surrender or liquidation. But this carries with it a cost.

A study for the Armed Forces of the Union noted in 2003 that '[t]he mental strain of having to fight one's own people is infinitely greater than fighting the enemy'.[65] It goes on to say that 'dilemma in being able to resolve the contradictions between general war and LIC, particularly concepts of "enemy", "objectives" and "minimum force" is one set of problems. The other being that 'in general war nation looks upon the soldier as a saviour, out here (during internal wars) he is at the receiving end of public hostility. Unable to understand these conflicting relations, the soldier is desensitized'.

But even more critical in such counter-insurgency wars is the role of the 'irregulars' on the side of the State such as the use of the so-called Home Guards against the Mau Mau guerrillas, self-defence committees against the Maoist insurgents in Peru, local Afghans against the Taliban forces, etc. Closer home in India, we have Special Police Officers, or SPOs, who operate under a variety of names in different war zones. Thus they are called 'Ikhwanis' in Jammu and Kashmir, SULFA in Assam – an acronym for the surrendered militant members of the United Liberation Front – Koya Commandos in Chhattisgarh or simply SPOs elsewhere. One of the major reasons for employing 'irregulars' as part of the military suppression of rebels is to create divisions, use them to carry out ruthless acts, or for gathering information for 'actionable intelligence', and also to send a message that it does not pay to challenge the State. The cost of doing so is high as instances abound in war zones of rape, molestation, massacre, destruction, looting, arrests and enforced disappearances. These 'government militants' provide a cover to the actual State forces to deny any involvement in war crimes by passing them off as a result of internecine conflict within the movement or as part of the resistance offered by the 'people' to the Maoist movement.

Alexander B. Downes captures this succinctly:

> States in today's world that are beset by civil conflict face conflicting pressures: the international community favours negotiations and power

> sharing, but governments also want to make as few concessions as possible to rebels. Using negotiations to create spoilers provides one way out of this dilemma: the government can co-opt certain groups into signing a superficial peace accord and then tar those who refuse to agree as intransigent dead-enders. The trick is to offer just enough in the way of concessions to peel away opportunistic or moderate rebel factions. In exchange for perks and material rewards, these groups can be enlisted to provide intelligence or additional combat power against their former comrades'.[66]

What this obviously does is to create a state of impunity for the security forces. If a rapist or a killer wanted by law or declared as an absconder by the Court is protected by the police who claim they cannot track him although he participates in raid-and-search operations and lives in the police camp, it is due to the fact that such a person is considered a 'hero' as such persons 'instill fear' by their 'ruthlessness'.[67]

What the Maoist movement confronts is an absolute war being prosecuted by the State where the rebels are projected as criminals. The dirty war conducted by the State makes the task of restraining the revolutionary forces against the provocative acts of the State forces a formidable challenge. So the demands we place on the revolutionary movement must be informed, if not tempered, by the actual conduct of war by the State forces.

But if the basic objective of the government's military suppression is to force the people to stop supporting the rebels, whereas that of the rebels is to retain popular backing, then it is incumbent upon the Maoists to avoid reckless and cruel conduct. Their military methods cannot be a mirror image of the State forces but actually must remain sharply different in its politics.

# 7

# Escalating War

In India, war preparations get euphemistically referred to as 'capacity building'. Thus, augmentation of manpower, escalation in war-making, and building up of war hysteria, carry on under the rubric of 'capacity building'. There are eighty-five battalions of Central Para Military Forces (CPMFs) trained along the line of the Indian Army's infantry formations. Skilled in jungle warfare, they are assisted by more than 100 battalions of State armed constabularies, the Indian Reserve battalions, and 27,363 Special Police Officers (SPO), backed by the armed Indian Air Force helicopters providing logistical help in combat. All of these forces are armed with lethal weapons in this new war terrain covering thirty-four districts across nine states of the Indian Union.

In order to prepare the way for eventual army engagement, four unified commands are being set up, which will be headed by the Chief Secretary, with a retired Major General acting as a security advisor to the respective state governments. The Indian Army chief has also asked his senior officers to be

> mentally prepared to step into the fight against Naxalism ... *It might be in six months or in a year or two* but if we have to maintain our relevance as a tool of the state, we will have to undertake things that the nation wants us to.[68] [Emphasis added.]

A one-page press note issued by the army headquarters says:

> This will be the first time that any sizable strength of the Army moves into this region. The deployment will indeed open up the region to the outside world. Purchase of local materials and supplies will bring jobs and finance to cash strapped villages. The presence of the Army will also bring feeling of security in the villages.[69]

Although the army refuses to engage in combat without the promulgation of AFSPA in the war against the Maoists, its footprint, however, is enlarging in the new war zone. The Army actually does not even need AFSPA because S197 of the CrPC read with S125 and 126 of the Army Act indemnify them. In any case, in Chhattisgarh, the army is setting up a sub-area or brigade headquarters in Raipur, a training facility in Bilaspur, and a battle manoeuvre range in Narayanpur (near Abhuj Maad forest) for which it has been given an area spread over 500 sq kms, something which is in violation of both the Fifth Schedule, Panchayat Extension to Schedule Area (1996) and the Forest Rights Act (2006). The army has sought 'Rules for Engagement' from the state government to meet the contingencies bound to arise since their battle range is deliberately located in the conflict zone.

Such is the level of 'capacity build-up' that Indian Air Force helicopters which carry troops, to and from the battle zones, or flies out the injured, come with Light Machine Gun-carrying commandos called Garuds.

A senior army officer told the *Asian Age* that

> there will not be any permanent camp for training in jungle warfare and counter-insurgency for Army personnel in Bastar. Jawans will (be) given training in temporary camps which will be shifted frequently to different locations in mountainous region of Bastar.[70]

But a senior police officer explained that

> the training grounds chosen are mostly in Maoist strongholds. Frequent movements of Army jawans in Bastar jungles, in course of their training, will put the Naxals under severe strain.[71]

Brigadier B.K. Ponwar, head of Counter-terrorism and Jungle Warfare College, Kanker, was virtually gloating when he asserted that

> [t]he Narayanpur base shall be located right next to the den of the Naxalites. It shall have a good psychological impact on the Naxalites to know that the tiger is sitting just outside.[72]

Thus, it's a matter of time before the army units start fighting yet another war at home.

A question arises: Maoists have been around for decades; what is it that lies behind the escalation of war since 2004–05? The Indian Prime Minister was candid about this with editors and publishers of newspapers and magazines. He told them on 6 September 2010 that

> Naxalite areas happen to be those areas which are heartland of India's mineral wealth . . . if we are not allowed to exploit the mineral resources of this country I think the growth path of this country will be adversely affected.

Thus the link between the war and the need to attract capital into the lucrative mining sector is not fanciful but real, as vouchsafed by the Indian PM himself.

Let us recall that the build-up towards this new phase of war against the Naxalites/Maoists began in 1998 when the Ministry of Home Affairs, under the Hindu right-wing party, Bharatiya Janata Party and headed by L.K. Advani began speaking about the security threat posed by the

Maoists/Naxalites. It was under his watch that reference was dropped about the socio-economic roots of the Naxalite rebellion.[73] This step led to their criminalization. The issue of land and land reforms, including that of giving land to the landless, has a long history and goes back to India's freedom struggle where peasant movements had raised the demand for land reforms and distribution as a key component of the democratic reform of the country post-transfer of power. Decoupling the socio-economic reality from the revolutionary movement was to develop into a project of war just as their criminalization was to rob the Maoists of their legitimacy as belligerents.

In 1999–2000, the annual report of the MHA shifted focus to 'plan and execute coordinated action to contain and ultimately eliminate the scourge of left wing extremist violence . . .' By the year 2002-03, the MHA annual report began to advocate assisting local vigilante groups against the Maoist movement. Reference to Maoists also became more strident. Within three months of the Congress-led United Progressive Alliance government coming to power in May 2004, i.e., on 11 August 2004, the MHA officials were briefing the members of the Standing Committee of Parliament on Home Affairs that Naxalites/Maoists pose even a 'bigger threat' than the 'Islamic fundamentalist groups'. It also became clear that there existed a consensus between the BJP and the Congress to wage war against the Maoists.

On 20 December 2007 at the Chief Ministers' conference on Internal Security, the Prime Minister of India in his opening speech raised the pitch when he said:

> As we survey the national security scenario, there are a few aspects which are cause of concern. I wish to highlight a few of them. . . . Just a few days ago, we had a major incident of a jailbreak in Chhattisgarh. This was not an isolated incident. Not a day passes

> without an incident of Left Wing Extremism taking place somewhere or the other. Over the last year, the activities of Naxal groups have revealed new aspects. They seem to have developed the capability in some areas to launch frontal attacks on police forces and establishments. They are certainly targeting all aspects of economic activity. They are targeting vital economic infrastructure so as to cripple transport and logistic capabilities and also slow down any development activity. This helps them sustain their ideology of deprivation and neglect. They have even managed to eliminate some important political leaders and their associates in some states.[74]

Therefore, the PM went on to say that 'we cannot rest in peace until we have eliminated this virus'. He said, '[W]e need to cripple the hold of Naxalite forces with all means at our command', adding that '[w]hile tackling Naxal groups militarily, we also need to choke their support infrastructure'. Although the PM pinned the blame on 'LWE' for slowing down economic activity in order to 'sustain their ideology', he remained silent over sixty years of 'deprivation and neglect' by successive Indian governments. Thus, suppressing this class war acquired the highest priority. Characterizing the Maoists as criminals or illegal belligerents was one way of enabling a bloody suppression. The operative keywords were 'cripple', 'eliminate', 'choke', etc. Thus once a party or an organization is proscribed, every activity carried out by their members or supporters becomes criminal. Worse, the combatants become illegal belligerents, nay criminals, who are robbed of their rights and privileges. Then, history, politics and motivations lose their significance. It is an 'absolute war' waged by the State that confronts the revolutionaries.

# 8

# People's War

Armed struggle by Communist revolutionaries in India has a long history, starting in 1946 with what is popularly called the Telangana Uprising, which lasted until 1951. After 1951, the then Communist Party surrendered its arms and participated in elections. However, sections of the party remained discontented with this policy shift. In 1966, with the Naxalbari uprising, some of these party veterans broke away and went on to form the CPI (ML). By the 1970s, the process of fragmentation of the movement began, only to stop towards the 1990s when those who still subscribed to armed struggle drew close, while those opposed to it began to participate in elections. Through a process of merger of parties emerged the CPI (Maoist) in 2004. Those who took to armed struggle opted for PPW as the path to be followed, believing that by capturing power in one area, i.e., ousting administration from an area – to begin with, a hilly forested area where the presence of the State is weak – and establishing a parallel rule, the revolutionaries could slowly expand and surround the towns – somewhat akin to, but not exactly replicating, what happened in China – and seize power.

According to the party's present position as delineated in its document *Strategy and Tactics of the Indian Revolution*, there are four principal characteristics of India's Revolutionary War:

(a) Uneven economic and political development and the semi-colonial and semi-feudal character of Indian Society;
(b) Enemy is big and powerful having centralized state machinery and well-equipped army;
(c) The Communist Party, the guerrilla army and the agrarian revolutionary movement in India are still weak; and
(d) Our country is a prison house of nationalities where some nationalities are engaged in bitter struggles against the Indian state to achieve their right to self-determination.[75] Therefore, the line of area-wise seizure of power through the strategy of protracted people's war has to be adopted basing on the relatively backward and strategic areas of the countryside.

Point (d) is a clear departure from the Chinese path in so far as the nationality struggle brings the Maoists much closer to the Leninist position on the nationality question, something the Chinese did not have to deal with or had little to offer to.

Side-stepping the characterization of the Indian State and Society and knowing that the designation of India as semi-colonial and semi-feudal is contested and challenged— and studies tend to suggest that in rural India class differentiation has been blunted by a preponderance of petty commodity production, self-employment of a large number of people, shrinking of farm size per household, etc.—the task of deciding who the allies are and who the enemy becomes more complex.

It is important to note that the party believes there are two types of revolutionary wars. They rule out applicability of what it considers suitable for a capitalist country where bourgeois democratic rights prevail and the 'party of the proletariat prepares the working class and its allies through open and legal struggles—parliamentary, trade union, general strikes, political agitation . . .' and such activities are used to organize a countrywide armed insurrection. It then goes on to say that the

> vastness of the countryside, the inadequacy of the transport and communication system and the isolation of the remote countryside from the military centres, and above all, the inadequacy of the reactionary forces in comparison to the vastness of the country and the population . . . can transform the vast tracts of the countryside into red resistance areas, guerrilla zones, guerrilla bases and liberated areas . . .[76]

So area-wise seizure of power is meant not only to hold on to a territory but also to expand spatially and bring other areas under control. Therefore, what they do as 'rulers' impacts their movement.

In an interview, the general secretary of the CPI (Maoist) opined that

> we are confident that there is an advantage in the long run which cannot be achieved in a short period . . . we want to stretch this war and transform the situation to our advantage favourable to the revolution.[77]

Thus, they expect to expand rapidly in the course of this war. This is not altogether unrealistic since they did manage to expand during the previous two occasions when military operations were launched against them in DK, as also in the Jangalmahal area of West Bengal and Dumka area of Jharkhand. Another Maoist leader had asserted

> [t]he Party and leadership will grow rapidly in times of war . . . War is giving birth to new generals and commanders, which we never anticipated in normal times. While it took several years to produce a leader

> of calibre in relatively peaceful times, it is taking a fraction of that time in the midst of the war situation.[78]

How realistic are these propositions?

While wars, conflicts and crises do sharpen people's powers of comprehension, and they also help to spread, in this case the Maoists' political appeal, it does not mean that political education of the cadres gets replaced by education through war. What it implies is that it becomes easier for people to understand unfolding developments and linkages between what appears to be disparate issues. For instance, CPI (Maoist) leaders told Jan Myrdal and me that when they used the word 'fascism' in the DK area prior to 2005, people could not grasp what it meant. However, no sooner did the State patronize the private militia Salwa Judum and begin its brutal campaign than it brought home to them what it was that the Maoists were warning them about. However, war can also cloud intelligence and trigger irrational and cruel behaviour unless political control is maintained. Also, precisely because war heightens the senses, civil wars in particular, which tend to be 'dirty wars', can also alienate sections of people due to weak articulation of the rebels' political objectives; other causes of alienation could be needless bloodletting, conflicting or divided loyalties (due to caste, religion, ethnicity, economic ties) and 'manipulative' mass political mobilization.

In order to understand, let us consider the actual situation first. A spate of crackdowns and arrests made by the security agencies in two years (2009 and 2010) in Uttar Pradesh, Bihar, Haryana, Gujarat, Maharashtra, Orissa and West Bengal does suggest that the Maoists suffered a setback. But it also showed how rapidly Maoists had spread in different parts of India. This was also the period when their critics were proved wrong in claiming that the Maoist PPW was going nowhere. In the Jangalmahal region of

West Bengal, they had managed to emerge as a strong fighting force of the people, just as they did in Dumka (Jharkhand). In purely politico-military terms, the meticulously planned looting of armouries as well as jail raids to free prisoners showed that they were capable of moving a force of 200–500 across a large territory, and train a team drawn from different units for several months, something not possible without a social base in those territories to plan and carry out operations. No longer were they a ragtag guerrilla band, the irregular or partisan of yore, but an army in the making. In all these areas, they were actively engaged in building public assets such as ponds and roads, while also forming teams to develop agriculture and to provide elementary health and education to people. This indeed contributed to pitching revolutionary transformation back on to the agenda. The spurt in reports of Maoist activities from Assam and Manipur in the recent months of 2011–12 suggests that they have expanded to new areas, despite suffering losses elsewhere. However, the forced retreat from Saranda forest in Jharkhand and the disarray in Jangalmahal in West Bengal needs to be explained.

In Saranda, 10,000 forest dwellers are being forced to settle in ten 'model' villages (strategic hamlets), and seventeen camps of central paramilitary forces are coming up in order to 'protect' the people from the Maoists and allow mining and mineral-based companies to exploit the mineral riches. In fact as a sign of things to come, the all-powerful Forest Advisory Committee has allowed for the diversion of 500 hectares of land falling under the Singhbhum Elephant Reserve in Saranda, in order to enable Jindal Steel and Power to start mining for iron ore.[79] In Jangalmahal of West Bengal, losses have been many: the cowardly murder of Kishenji who headed the Eastern

Regional Bureau of the party; custodial killings of scores of middle-ranking cadres; arrests of nearly 300 members and supporters; enforced surrender (where children and parents are used as 'bait') of around 20 cadres; and the disbanding of several guerrilla squads. All this has ensured the shrinking of the guerrilla zone. So they are weaker today than they were a few years ago.

Thus, offering armed resistance over a prolonged period of time in order to seize power also means that war does not progress in a linear fashion but goes through ups and downs, of lull and storm, ebb and flow. It also does not mean that the withdrawal of Maoist guerrillas from one area means defeat, because a tactical retreat is not the same thing as defeat; but nor can losses incurred, say in West Bengal, be brushed aside as temporary or partial loss. It is the concrete conditions that must be understood. Conditions within India vary from one place to another just as they do among the seventy-eight districts where Maoists are said to be relatively strong, and 548 districts where they are not. In these days, the penetration of the Indian State or its administrative reach is over a much larger territory and its *absence* confined to a shrinking area as imperialist globalization seeks newer and cheaper sources of resources and comes into conflict with those who are fighting to retain their common resources. This has thrown up the slogan shared across the entire resistance in India 'to resist land grab' by the corporations, which is a marked shift from the earlier popular slogan asking the landless and the land-poor to 'grab land'. So how much of this changing reality has been factored in by the Maoists? Because it is no longer a case of being isolated from the Centre or limited reach of central power—the State has, in fact, increased penetration and widened its hold. Surely, a military strategy must keep in pace with this changing social and political reality? This is where absence of urban strategy is felt acutely. For instance, instead of encircling the urban areas by capturing power in the countryside, there is a danger that it is the Maoists′ forest strongholds which are getting encircled. So the idea of encirclement needs to be looked at again. This does not mean that the Maoists' armed struggle is unsuited to circumstances prevailing in some parts of the country; rather, it throws up the need to combine different forms of struggle, that is, one where guerrilla activities in the countryside as well as in the urban areas are combined, just as much as armed and mass struggles are both required. Let me begin by examining the current strategy of the armed struggle.

# 9
# Challenges of Marking Territories

The concept of 'area-wise seizure of power' presupposes Communist revolutionaries dominating an area where they control the territory and run a parallel administration. But it is one thing to dominate forested hilly areas, where political and social diversity is less pronounced than to dominate non-forested plains where the politics and social diversity is more complex Another key precept of the 'area-wise seizure of power' is to hold on to territory. To prepare for revolutionary upheaval, it is important to build bases as firmly as possible, and to move to other areas when it is not possible to hold on to an area. But this presupposes that the conditions would be similarly suitable in other parts of India. In other words, the very circumstance that legitimizes partisan war in one region, and the absence of similar conditions in others, makes it difficult to conceive of a uniform approach. For instance, how will they capture, let alone consolidate, their hold over territories in the plains with their more advanced social relations of production? Besides, militarily, they are weak; their numbers are modest. This means that they have to be mindful of their politics. It is not guns that fight but people wielding guns who fight. The limited armed strength of the Maoists gets enhanced many times over because of the mass support. Conversely, if people's support gets eroded, their firepower diminishes. Thus a strategy which works in one area may not work elsewhere.

If it is inherent in the objective of 'area-wise seizure of power' to expand to new areas, the question is what should be the nature of such an expansion; this involves looking at the equation between the party units and the guerrilla squads, and the balance between political mobilization and guerrilla activities. In an 'area-wise seizure', the needs of the war or demands of the struggle area often prevail over other considerations; for example, where urban areas act as a 'supply chain', i.e., providing cadres, resulting in depletion in ranks of activists who work in urban areas, it is bound to weaken the movement in urban areas. Besides, when 'area-wise seizure of power' takes place in places isolated from each other rather than a countryside encircling a city, the territories held by the Maoists also get isolated and encircled.

Although the Communist Party of India (Maoist) is banned, the Maoists control territories where they run a parallel administration. Thus they are both, so to say, outlaws as well as rulers. For instance, in central India, called the Dandakaranya, all development is now the responsibility of the people's government, i.e., the Janatam Sarkar. The established administration is being replaced by the strengthening of the people's government. The Revolutionary People's Committees (RPCs) are elected by people above the age of eighteen every three years. Fifteen villages with population anywhere between 500–3000 make up an RPC. These RPCs elect members to Area RPCs which comprise between 3–5 RPCs. In turn, 3 ARPCs constitute a Division RPC.

But the movement is not a monolith. Some areas are more organized such as DK than Bihar-Jharkhand. For instance, the area-level organs of power, ARPCs, have been set up in DK but not elsewhere. Similarly, '[e]xcept in DK, in other areas the growth of people's militia is not significant', says the Political Organizational Report of the CPI (Maoist), presented at the 9th Congress (2007). This is true, it adds, for grassroots-level organization as well. There are other differences too. For instance, in the Bastar region of DK where land was distributed, the ousted landlords have not been able to either sell or retake possession of the lands expropriated from them and distributed to the poor tribals by the Peoples Government (Janatam Sarkar, JS). In Andhra Pradesh, agricultural land, nearly 1,00,000 acres, distributed by the party lay fallow because the police and civil authorities made sure that the Dalits, in particular, who became owners of the land did not get to cultivate those fields. Or, if they did, that the harvest was destroyed. Meanwhile, attempts were made by the landlords to sell off the land which was then thwarted through guerilla-squad action instead of mass mobilization. This practice of squads carrying out preventive actions against land takeover and overemphasis on armed actions, which replaced mass mobilization, probably contributed to the decline in the movement in Andhra Pradesh.

In DK, during the peak of SJ, these lands may have remained fallow, but by 2007 onwards, Adivasi peasants began to return to cultivate the lands, and the size of the land that's fallow gradually shrunk. Ousted landlords who joined SJ to wreak havoc dared not reoccupy their lands. In Bastar, JS extends credit and seeds to poor peasants and loans to purchase bullocks so as to encourage the peasants to take to ploughing their fields with them rather than using shovels. Besides, in DK's JS areas there are no arrack shops and only traditional liquor is brewed. Therefore, mobilizing women against arrack shops, so effective in the eighties phase of the movement in Andhra Pradesh, is not needed here. Moreover, incidence of alcoholism is far less common in DK. As for the punishment that is meted out, it is not in excess of the mistake committed; in fact, people there express pride in the fact that ordinary crimes have reduced.

Seizure of power in areas that are far apart tends to compel decentralization where the party units and guerrillas of different regions work with a lot more autonomy. That is not a problem in itself. The problem arises when this lessening of central control carries on down to the squad level, resulting in the loosening of discipline and dilution of politics. A document called *New Circular on Rectification* is significant in this regard.[80] Rectification campaigns are the means by which the party identifies the faults and shortcomings of its party members and units.

The most important thing to note is the criticism against relying on squad action alone, instead of mass mobilization, to deal with class issues in the areas dominated by the party. The political report of the 9th Congress of the CPI (Maoist) expressed concern that there were areas where grassroots party organization is weak with insignificant party units at the village level. Some states have formed party units at the village level but they are non-functional. In many areas the party activity is still *squad centred*. This makes the masses passive supporters and dependent on the squads for taking up struggles and in solving the issues at the village level.

It has to be mentioned here that loss of territory need not be a major deterrent against PPW, if the subjective forces remain intact. But it does cause a problem if in their area of control either the subjective forces are weak or are themselves a cause for concern.

A report from the Bihar-Jh Special Area Committee on 'Rectification' is a candid indictment of certain practices that has emerged in *some* areas.

Among the recommendations, the report calls for ensuring that the party members do not accept any 'obligation from contractors' unless it is 'first discussed in the committee concerned'.[81] It calls for warning and then expulsion of cadres found to be violating the party's directive against hobnobbing with the contractors and middlemen unless authorized, within limits set by the higher committees.

This report was issued immediately after the formation of the CPI (Maoist) and refers to the presence of contractors and middlemen causing a problem in some areas of Jharkhand. What we do not know is whether this trend has been rectified. Even if such problems are 'local', it does impact the overall PPW because Jharkhand, Chhattisgarh and Orissa are the three states where the Maoists are the strongest. Moreover, any problem that crops up in one area does overall affect the PPW.

# 10

# When Politics Is Not in Command

What does 'politics must command the gun' mean? Should not wars be fought by soldiers without being shackled by politics?

Revolutionary war, by its very nature, is a self-consciously political project. It is this that must act to restrain the war from degenerating into bloodletting and of getting unhitched from popular support.

In the Niyamat Ansari case, in response to criticism by civil liberties groups in India, the Bihar-Jharkhand-North Chhattisgarh-UP Territorial Regional Committee issued an apology, on 1 September 2011. It claims that there were charges against Niyamat Ansari for grabbing land and benefitting a section of the villagers. So was this a case where a section of the people aligned or close to the party was upset because Niyamat Ansari allowed forest land to be grabbed for a consideration when he had been warned not to do so because of the tension in the village over this? Was it a case of the party standing by the most marginalized tribals, or was the decision to act against Niyamat Ansari a move to warn others not to defy the party order about forest grab? A press release issued on 3 September, this time by Koyal Shankh Zonal Committee of the CPI-Maoist, through its spokesperson Dinbandhu, says that

> [Niyamat Ansari] was killed not because of his role as an MGNREGA activist, but because he along with his associate, one Bhukhan Singh, was found guilty of capturing forest land in Jerua village for agricultural purpose for which he was subjected to beating.

But a statement issued by several social activists on 29 April 2011 titled 'Fairy Tales about Niyamat' points out that

> [d]uring the last few years, 86 families in Kope, including Bhukhan and Niyamat, have been trying to establish claims on local forest land under the Forest Rights Act. This was part of a larger movement in Latehar District, spearheaded by Bharat Jan Andolan and the Campaign for Survival and Dignity. It was, however, opposed by the upper castes and other well-off people of Kope (who had not occupied forest land and would not get any direct benefits), led by the same gang of corrupt contractors who were looting NREGA funds. As pointed out by Fr George Monippally, local convenor of Bharat Jan Andolan, for them this was just another way of 'retaliating' against Bhukhan and Niyamat. For instance, it is unlikely to be a coincidence that the (so-called) 'Van Suraksha Samiti' (Forest Protection Committee) formed by the Forest Department and dominated by the upper castes (even in a tribal majority village) in response to this movement lodged a malicious FIR against Bhukhan, Niyamat and others in this matter at the precise time when the contractors were under the scrutiny of an NREGA Lok Adalat, in February 2009. Incidentally, the same process of staking claims on forest land, and verification of claims as per Forest Rights Act, was taking place in many other villages in Manika Block and Latehar District.

So the difference between the two versions is vast and not miniscule.

While the actual facts could be contentious, what is abundantly clear is that punishment exceeded the crime committed and Niyamat Ansari's death due to beating cannot be washed away as an instance of 'accident'. Although the party's apology statement, welcome in so far as they reveal the intention of the party to atone for this crime, it does not explain why in an area they regard as a guerrilla zone, with shifting control between the guerrilla and the State forces, they could not hold a People's Court, how the differences with social activists turned antagonistic, and how facts could remain a matter of dispute.

The support extended by the party for the guerrilla massacre of eleven poor tribals, including women and children, with injury to fifty others and thirty-six houses burnt down at the Phulwaria-Kudasi (Korasi) village in Jamui district of Bihar, on 17 February 2010, reflects the absence of political control over guns. A bigger problem is, however, the partial mobilization of the poor in the area. Kudasi village is inhabited by backward communities such as Kodas, Santhals and Sahs, along with Yadavs. While Maoists are present in the forests close by, there remain several villages here which are not under their sway and Kudasi is considered as an anti-Naxal village because the Koda tribals are the beneficiary of a watershed programme; it was a member of their community who was elected to be the chief of the Panchayat. Schism between the local communities and the Maoists was also reflected in the killing on 2 July 2011 of a tribal assistant sub-inspector Lukas Tete, one of the four police personnel taken as hostage by the Maoists, while three other Yadav sub-inspectors were set free. Thus this divide is much deeper and probably of a long vintage. However, the village was visited by guerrilla squads occasionally when they travelled through it on their way to somewhere else. The reason for the hostility is not exactly known, but the composition of the Maoist cadres in this area are predominately Yadavs/Ravidasis, etc., and this could have contributed to the divide and hostility. While the mobilization of people to fight for justice does remain a very important objective for the Maoists, it appears that exigencies of war make the issue of survival too very important. Could this have pushed the Maoists, for the sake of their own protection, to make a choice to favour the non-tribals who dominate the area, and did this then contribute to making the Koda tribals distrustful and fearful of the Maoists whom they saw as being close to non-tribals or caste Hindus? Whatever the reason, some Koda tribals, from among whom Special Police Officers are also recruited, chose to inform the police, who laid a trap and killed the Maoists, and spread the story that it was the tribal villagers who had attacked and killed them. While the police may have chosen to blame the tribals in order to take advantage of the situation and sow division, as also to make it appear that the villagers are opposing the Maoists, it brought upon the tribals the wrath of the Maoists.

Clausewitz says:

> [T]he political object', 'as the original motive of the War, will be the standard for determining both the aim of the military force and also the amount of effort to be made. This it cannot be in itself, but it is so in relation to both the belligerent States, (or parties) because we are concerned with realities, not with mere abstractions. One and the same political object may produce totally different effects upon different people, or even upon the same people at different times; we can, therefore, only admit the political object as the measure, by considering it in its effects

> upon those masses which it is to move, and consequently the nature of those masses also comes into consideration.[82]

If the presence of the party in the area, and the espousal of its politics meant to protect and encourage the poor to organize themselves for their own emancipation, gets stunted, then divisions among the poor results in them occupying opposing sides. It is this that creates the fissure that can end up harming the movement. If the party claims it is against mindless acts of violence, then commission of such acts by the party itself means either that its armed squads are not guided by the politics of emancipation or that its politics is getting reduced to settling scores in some places, rather than neutralizing the hostility of a section through politics. A basic principle of revolutionary guerrilla warfare is that politics must control the guns and not vice versa. Revolutionary movements rely on their mass work and political appeal to win over people. So the question is, why and how did they fail to do so in Jamui? Why and how could Niyamat Ansari carry out his alleged forest grab to benefit a section of the people when evidence to this had not been provided? This goes to the heart of the problem.

Obviously, it is not the case that this problem is manifest in the entirety of the guerrilla zone in equal intensity. It is also not the case that the party cannot learn from its mistakes. The very fact that they admit to these faults somewhere accords them the capacity to be self-critical. And also a capacity to self-correct. But I suspect that recurring incidents of the squads taking matters into their own hands, and summary trials and executions, mean serious lapse in political control, and increase in arbitrary acts, which mark a breakdown in discipline. Refer to the excerpts from the document on 'Rectification' and the reference to squad action as replacing political mass action, something that has been frequently occurring. This means that the party has to learn to respect those who work among people, whether as reformers or revolutionaries, and who need not be in agreement with the Maoist ideology or programme. As they draw close to industrial townships or urban areas or plain rural areas, the Maoists have no choice but to acknowledge that their ideological hegemony will be contested; and if they can navigate themselves responsibly in such contexts, then it can result in a political leap forward.

In Jangalmahal scores of members belonging to the Communist Party (Marxist) were executed. Were these executions carried out after the higher courts/committees/instances upheld the conviction? Did the higher instances apply their mind? Did they consider the implications of killing an ordinary cadre belonging to the antagonist party? Of course, it is true that a political activist is not necessarily a paragon of virtue or always to be regarded as a non-combatant. A school teacher activist belonging to a political party could as well be a land broker, petty contractor, plunderer of resources meant for the people, or a police informer whose information results in killings of civilians and Maoist cadres. The local population certainly could be a better judge of his/her character and role. The Maoists cannot be oblivious to the need to be circumspect and should realize that bloodletting could rebound on them and create a constituency of aggrieved people whose antipathy towards them could be exploited by the government.

Thus, just as partial mobilization polarizes the local society, and the party is seen as standing by one group of people against the other, it undercuts its capacity to mobilize the majority of the oppressed. Similarly, targeting or cruelly carrying out the execution of, say, a CPI (M) cadre can backfire on the Maoists, as did happen in reality. A principle of guerrilla warfare is that a tactical error by either the guerrilla or the government forces can cause strategic loss and aggrieve many people. Just as punishing a local tyrant wins them accolades, wrongful punishment or a cruelly carried out execution can earn opprobrium and cause immense harm to the Maoist movement. In this context for the party GS to defend the Jamui massacre in December 2010 is astounding:

> In the Jamui incident, a reactionary gang sponsored by the government had caught eight of our comrades in Phulwaria-Kodasi village and killed them in the most heinous, brutal manner by chopping off their limbs. When such incidents happen, we will never be able to safeguard our movement or our people if we keep quiet and do not act. That was why we were compelled to counter-attack. In this attack, nine people died including three main *goonda* leaders. It is extremely sad that a woman and a child were caught in flames and had died accidentally. All the other seven were hard-core criminals, killers and lumpen elements. Our Bihar-Jharkhand Special Area Committee had issued a clear statement on this. It was published in the Bihar papers and in the Maoist Information Bulletin-17.

So an act can be justified as a 'counter-attack' on the ground of safeguarding the movement.

# 11
# When Simmer Turns into Boil

The pent-up fury of the oppressed, as Azad too had opined in his interview, is at times difficult to contain, accepting also that the urban middle-class perception could vary from that of the oppressed and the exploited who are simmering with suppressed rage at the gross injustices to which they are subjected. But the Jamui massacre cannot be explained away as a consequence of a dirty war wherein people kill each other or as the necessity of one massacre for another. What the killing represents points to a more critical lapse. While the footprint of the guerrillas is large, the political presence of the party does not necessarily match this. The absence of party units at the village level in some areas was observed by the 9th Party Congress, as mentioned earlier. The presence or absence of the party unit is not a 'mechanical' thing. It is in fact of political significance because the task of mobilizing people, carrying on work designed to help 'people's economy', ensuring participation of the people in the task of improving their economy, and inspiring them to join the party and become a guerrilla, etc., are not possible without the presence of party units.

Wars, in particular civil wars, are brutal and cruel. Experience shows that 'goodness' is not reciprocated by the government forces and agencies. The Maoists have risked much and lost much more each time they have come forward for a dialogue. Again and again, the State has betrayed and violated its pledges, its own laws and negotiated agreements. The execution of Maoist leader Azad deputed for talks with the central government-appointed mediator, Swami Agnivesh, the torture and killing of Kishenji when efforts were on in the state government of West Bengal to start a dialogue, the refusal of the Odisha government to implement its part of the negotiated agreement—an agreement that had resulted in the Maoists unilaterally releasing the abducted district collector, R. Vineet Krishna—the indifferent attitude towards releasing more than 644 tribals arrested on trumped-up charges because they dared to raise questions about land grab, their displacement, and the lukewarm attitude towards other demands all show that manipulation has become the second nature of the Indian State. This lends credence to what Sumanta Bannerjee once said:

> such generosity (releasing hostages, especially government officials) was being wasted on a ruthless enemy and at a terrible cost. It was like nursing back a dying snake to life, only to be bitten by it.[83]

Thus, when one pushes the Maoists to accept the Geneva Conventions, especially its common Article 3 and Protocol II which apply to the conduct of wars not international in nature, could one be exposing them to the 'venomous bites' of the State?

Let us consider the issue of executions. The Maoists claim to have a Constitution for their JS. Under its Article 5(a), certain guidelines are laid down for carrying out a death sentence. It says that before the People's Court 'implements death sentence the local people's government have to obtain permission from the higher courts'. Thus, summary executions and arbitrary acts were sought to be contained. However, both Jharkhand-Bihar and West Bengal have reported a spurt in summary executions.

The killing of CPM activists in Jangalmahal too does not escape this injunction. By the Maoists' own account, fifty-two CPM members were killed in just the first seven months of 2009, nearly two a week.[84] It is claimed by the former ruling party, the CPM, that in three years, 2009 to 2011, 210 of their members were killed by the Maoists.[85] Whatever be the figure, the question is: what were the charges against those who had been executed? Failure to provide any information means that we have only anecdotal explanations that these were all cruel and corrupt, so-called 'people's enemy', but there is no documented account available in the public domain. So how do we know if the killings of CPM members were actually the execution of *political opponents* or the annihilation of *informers* who had committed heinous crimes? For a leader of the party to suggest that lack of jails in Jangalmahal contributed to the killings, unlike in Dandakaranya, hints at the fact that while they did expand politically and geographically, they made up for the absence of their political hegemony in the contentious zone by recourse to force. Thus, their control was not just contentious but also weak. The Maoists appeared to be oblivious to the need to be circumspect, and seemed to have overlooked the fact that bloodletting would rebound on them and create a constituency of aggrieved people. For the government forces, kinship and other affiliations can become fertile ground for mobilizing sections of people who are hostile towards the rebels.

Going by the Maoists' own argument of PPW and 'area-wise seizure of power', it means that they believe they will be engaged in a long-drawn-out war. Revolutionary wars are meant to free the people from their shackles and allow their creative energies to flourish. Thus, revolutionaries cannot emulate the State forces, who by the very nature of counter-insurgency warfare fight a war of suppression, which is a dirty war made up of massacres, arson, looting, rapes, disappearances, torture, all aimed to terrorize the people into submission or to snap their links with the rebels. Nor can revolutionaries fight on the principle of reciprocity.

If we look carefully, in the areas where the party was confident about expanding it now sees its prospect coming under threat. Instead of expanding, there has been a shrinkage both in terms of losing areas of influence as well as in terms of depletion in the ranks of their political cadres because of killings and arrests. These arrests of party leaders and cadres is not only because of 'informers' and intelligence agencies determinedly pursuing them but also a manifestation of a problem, namely, erosion of their mass base and declining mass struggles in areas where the party was once dominant. Party cadres admit privately that it has become easier for the government agencies to nab their cadres and leaders because earlier they could move around somewhat freely because of mass struggles and their mass base, which provided the best protection, and that its absence has isolated them, with shelters getting fewer and so movement becoming riskier. These guerrillas can now survive only as 'fish in water'.

# 12
# Limits of Armed Struggle

So, is there a limit to the political objectives that can be achieved through an armed struggle in contemporary India? Or is it that while armed struggle is necessary, it is not a sufficient condition?

When the party expelled some members in Karnataka for refusing to initiate armed actions in the Malnad area of Western Ghat because the dissidents held that Malnad, with its developed agriculture and well linked to the outside world, offered the possibility of working 'lawfully' or at least invited another political approach, it was not just a question of party discipline but of an approach based on a concrete situation. The question right now is not whether they were right or wrong; the issue is of appreciating the concrete conditions on the ground.

This question arises out of trying to reconcile the understanding that 'mass organizations and mass struggles should serve the war between people's armed forces and enemy's forces once it has broken out, or, should be oriented towards the preparation for war' with the admonition that 'armed struggle cannot achieve success unless it is coordinated with other forms of struggle . . . This will amount to leaving behind masses and going ahead with only the advanced sections'.[86] Even when war takes precedence, People's War is not just about military combat but also about the political objective behind it since this war is also a way to mobilize, organize and make conscious the exploited classes of their condition and their historic responsibility as they struggle to seize power.

Take the Jangalmahal area of West Bengal as an example. As in other parts of West Bengal, the rule of CPM (1977–2011) was initially marked by 'Operation Bargadar', where the rights of tenant farmers and sharecroppers were protected, and agricultural labour saw a rise in wages, while political prisoners were released unconditionally. The recognition of Maoists/Naxalites, etc., as political prisoners also lent a degree of legitimacy to the belligerents. But the reforms gave way to the consolidation of CPM's control, and the local CPM units began to dominate both the administration and the local police stations so much so that they became the arbiters of work, wage, sale and purchase of land. Simultaneously, they prevented any other party from working in the villages that they controlled. In an interview, a senior Maoist leader pointed out that in 1998, when the statutory minimum wage rate was Rs 85 per day, people in Jangalmahal would receive Rs 22. When some groups raised the demand to raise it by Rs 3, i.e., to Rs 25, this was opposed by the local CPM units. As a result, overground mobilization work for Maoists thereafter became difficult.[87]

Maoists had been working among the tribals in Jangalmahal since 1994. The Maoist Communist Centre, which in 2004 merged with CPI (ML) PW to form the CPI (Maoist), began its political work in 1960s from the Jangalmahal area bordering the present-day state of Jharkhand. The area in fact was also a scene of a celebrated peasant uprising in early 1970s, known as the Gopiballavpur-Debra Uprising. A number of revolutionary parties have been active here. When the struggle for a separate Jharkhand state picked up in the 1980s, it found some resonance here, giving a boost to identity politics. A revolutionary formation, CPI (ML) PCC has been working here for several decades and it spearheaded the demand for an autonomous council for Jangalmahal, following the emergence of Jharkhand state in 2000. Meanwhile, the activities of the Maoists had also picked up.

In 1997–98, CPI (ML) PW had come to the aid of the ruling CPM near Jangalmahal, in what is called the Garbeta-Keshpur-Arambagh area, where pitched battles were being fought by the local CPM against the Trinamool Congress. A Maoist leader, in an interview, said,

> I myself had bought 5000 cartridges from the CPI (M) office. Where would the minister Susanta Ghosh be now had we not been there?[88]

This presumably won them the elbow room to consolidate their presence in the area. The administration began to take notice of this and in 2002, raids were conducted to 'nip the People's War-Maoist Coordination Centre, in the bud'. Arrest and sexual exploitation of Adivasis were common in the name of hunting down the PW-MCC.[89] It was reported in the media that people were told to either join the ruling CPM or the Jharkhand Party, or else, they were warned, they would be seen as belonging to the underground PW-MCC. By 2003, it was also being reported in Kolkata newspapers that Maoists were running schools for Adivasi children. But the movement shot into prominence on 2 November 2008 when an abortive attempt was made to assassinate the head of the Government of West Bengal. Following the bomb blast, the police cracked down on Adivasi villagers and caused the emergence of 'Peoples Committee Against Police Atrocities' (PCAPA) in which a number of radical and pro-people forces were represented. The demand for police personnel to come before the tribal assembly and beg forgiveness for crimes committed by them against the people acquired a life of its own, with the expulsion of the police and the administration from the Lalgarh area; then the PCAPA began running the administration.

At its height, the Jangalmahal struggle encompassed 1100 villages across a 1000 sq km area, and was organized under 150 Gram Committees (GCs) in Lalgarh and Belpahari blocks. Each GC represented several villages. Each GC comprised men and women in equal proportion. While Maoists were the dominant force, there were other political tendencies and groups present in the PCAPA. Concurrently, a solidarity movement, Lalgarh Solidarity Manch, grew in the urban areas of West Bengal and among students, intellectuals and other sections, thus the appeal of the Maoist party grew. But so did new challenges. Very early in 2008, Maoists were confronted with a party which too traced its root to the Naxalbari uprising of the 1960s. The Maoists opposed the Santosh Rana-led CPI (ML) for pushing ahead with the demand for an autonomous council for Jangalmahal within the state of West Bengal; such a move, they said, would promote tribal identity politics or play into the hands of the Left Front government.[90] They also accused Rana's party of covertly extending support to the vigilante groups being promoted by the ruling CPM. When Santosh Rana expressed willingness to accept an independent inquiry to establish the veracity of the charge of covert support for vigilantes, the Maoist party did not show much interest.

As a matter of principle, Maoists do not oppose identity struggles. The CPI (Maoist) document, 'Tactics and Strategy of Indian Revolution' states that 'the Party should organise Adivasis with the slogans, *'Right over the forest belongs to people and Adivasis*', '*Political Autonomy to the Adivasi territories*' and transform the territory as exploitation-free territory, i.e., 'red land', 'don't be divided, be united', 'unite the real friends against the real enemies', 'right over all the resources including water, forest etc.', 'right for protecting their own culture and development', and draw up a specific plan for work among them to mobilize them against economic, political, social and cultural oppression.'[91] However, they were right in emphasizing that the 'divisions' among the tribals should neither be lost sight of nor was it correct to essentialize tribal identity and underplay class divisions and struggle. The lessons of DK tend to confirm the correctness of this approach. Revolutionary movements are not wedded just to the issues of forest rights, opposition to land grab by corporations, and the displacement of people and loss of livelihood. They go beyond by bringing the focus on to the issue of 'political power'. The CPI (Maoist) was clear that the struggle in Jangalmahal was a struggle of the common people, initiated by the tribals and not a tribal identity struggle per se.

In Dandakaranya, the earliest struggles were mass-based, taking up issues like increasing tendu leaf collection rates, enforcing forest rights by chasing away corrupt forest officials, occupying cultivable lands in the forests and expropriation of land of the traditional chiefs.[92] The party's mass base grew from these struggles. In contrast in Jangalmahal, hardly had the struggle to raise tendu leaf rates spread than it got increased by a fiat of the armed squads. The fight against police atrocity attracted large gatherings of people, but there was little information about the mode of occupation of large plots of land, either public land or land in possession of the CPM apparatchiks. There were also no large landlords in this area. Thus, while a political programme based on primary demands like land, water, forest rights and employment, and mass struggles to implement them too emerged, it did not become a prominent part of the political work. This might have been more effective in exposing and isolating the CPI (M) rather than the recourse to individual killings.

A senior Maoist leader justified these killings by claiming that those were not normal conditions but conditions of war where the rules were different. He also said that

> [i]n order to tire out informers, the people are adopting a number of methods. On the other side, the state is also trying everything in its power to whet their greed. Thus the number of informers being killed is also mounting. *Had there been some proper system in Jangal Mahal today, the number of informers getting killed would have been far less. In different parts of Dandakaranya, informers are being detained in people's prisons.*[93] [Empasis added.]

It is true that in conditions of war, overground activities become difficult to carry out. Also, the difference between combatants and non-combatants becomes decisive, and informers or couriers are counted as combatants. However, the point is that the Maoists failed to grasp that such killings would carry repercussions where questions would be raised and charges of recklessness create fissures with 'friends'.

The absence of jails is not as important as the fact that in the first place, their domination of Jangalmahal was weak. An increase in the killing of 'informers' was co-related to the diktat issued to the CPM members in Jangalmahal to quit PCAPA or face social boycott. It may be true that the CPM local units and members worked as informers but the diktat also enabled both the CPM, then the ruling party in the province, and the military forces, to find a way to infiltrate

PCAPA. A combination of these factors may have contributed to a spurt in informer killings. However, the recent killing of Babu Bose, a former member of the CPM-led vigilante group who switched allegiance to TC, shows that without politically isolating the ruling TC (as earlier the CPM), his killing only strengthened the resolve of his followers to wreak revenge.[94] Furthermore, without politically isolating the CPM or TC through a popular political campaign, the increased killings actually eroded the Maoist appeal and fractured the urban solidarity movement. War fought by revolutionaries cannot adopt the same approach as that followed by other belligerents. The ethical rules of war and their observance by the revolutionaries are essential to promote their politics and rally real and potential friends and allies.

Another mistake was in publicly declaring that they had built and controlled the movement in Jangalmahal. This ran counter to working secretly or in 'non-open' ways because of the compulsion on the ground where the Maoist party is criminalized. This public 'ownership' proved to be a political miscalculation and subverted the PCAPA's emergence as a mass movement representing diverse political forces, even when Maoists remained the dominant force.[95] What it also did was to undermine the open leadership of the PCAPA, pushing the CPI (Maoist) cadres to the forefront. The emergence of PCAPA was an achievement. The work carried out by them in the field of health, education, small irrigation projects to benefit peasants, the help provided to small and marginal farmers, participation of women, etc., were remarkable contributions in a short span, despite all-out efforts by the state administration and the military forces to thwart such activities, as in by physically closing down health centres and schools or simply stopping doctors and teachers from entering these areas. All this held out the promise of providing the Maoists with a mass organization for mass popular action and effectively getting around the proscription on them which prevented them from open political work. The urge to take credit and claim leadership of the movement widened the rift in the united effort comprising diverse political persuasions and made the Maoist control of the PCAPA a divisive issue in Jangalmahal. This also lent weight to the propaganda of the CPM-led Left Front government in West Bengal and the UPA government at the Centre that the PCAPA was nothing but a Maoist front. This cleared the way for joint forces operation, when precisely for this reason and knowing well that such an offensive was imminent no sooner than the elections to the fifteenth Parliament in India (May 2009) were over, they ought to have ensured that the united front remained intact. This failure contributed to the erosion of Maoist appeal both within and outside Jangalmahal, and by the time the 2011 elections to the state assembly drew close, conditions on the ground had altered.

This was reflected in the confusion among PCAPA over whether to participate in the elections, support the Trinamool Congress or stay out by boycotting the polls. These divisions and confusion helped the Trinamool Congress, which won four of the five seats from Jangalmahal. Thus, whereas in the May 2009 parliamentary elections, voting percentage was less than 10 per cent, in the 2011 May assembly elections, the voting percentage crossed 60 per cent. What does this imply? That there was no poll boycott campaign in the 2011 polls by the Maoists, unlike in the 2009 parliamentary elections when the Maoists' boycott call was effective and voting was at below 10 per cent? Or that in the 2011 polls, they encouraged people to vote for the TC? Or that the difference in voter turnout in 2009 and 2011 reflects loss of ground for the Maoists since the heydays of 2009?

But a larger issue is posed. The charge and counter-charge against the Maoists for having supported the TC—to the extent that they campaigned even against the jailed leader of PCAPA Chatrathar Mahato—brought out an old problem which confronts them even today. What should be the approach towards elections during the PPW? If there's a tactical bending of policy as regards election boycott, what would be better: to support one ruling class alliance against another or encourage those who are part of a mass movement to stand for elections? In the 2004 elections in Andhra Pradesh, the Maoist Party was accused of conducting a campaign with the slogan 'Smash Telugu Desam Party and the Bharatiya Janata Party', which ended up assisting the Congress party to sweep the assembly elections. In West Bengal, the main slogan was to 'Defeat the CPM'.

Remarkably, neither in Andhra Pradesh in 2004 or West Bengal in 2011 were so-called peace talks contingent upon Maoists either backing the Congress or the Trinamool Congress in the elections. It was their own calculations that pushed them, tacitly if not overtly, to support one ruling-class party over another. And consider the decimation of the rank and file of Maoists in Andhra Pradesh in 2004–05 at the hands of the very same Congress party whom they had tacitly supported. They ought not to have ignored the likelihood of the repeat of the same in West Bengal. In Jangalmahal, the arrest and killings of Maoist cadres could be traced to their easy identification by the Trinamool Congress members. Both experiences compel the Maoists to take another look at their elections policy. In West Bengal, they could have encouraged PCAPA to put up candidates as a way of enhancing their own political appeal as well as to ensure that the TC did not get to replace the CPM and consolidate themselves in Jangalmahal.

# 13

# Blame Game or Learning from Mistakes

It was under Kishenji's leadership that the CPI (Maoist) emerged from the shadows of armed resistance into open mass politics in West Bengal. Some of the features that helped in such a consolidation were: the mass mobilization and constitution of Peoples Committee against Police Atrocities, enhanced role for women through the formation of the Nari Izzat Bachao Committee with their open rallies and other forms of agitation. The other aspect had to do with the developmental activities that were carried out by mobilizing Adivasis and other peasantry. What all this did was to offer the Maoists a possibility of breaking out of the straitjacket of either armed or mass struggle by linking one to the other. Thus, the initial surge offered possibilities to Maoists of playing an active role in open politics.

This was no mean achievement for a movement which after the Naxalbari uprising had remained on the fringes of politics in West Bengal. The energy and enthusiasm generated was such that even the urban classes could not remain immune to its appeal.

But the speed with which its decline came about points towards how the initial prospects got eroded, if not botched, by mistakes that were committed on the way. From being able to move freely in Jangalmahal to being on the run embodies this trajectory. Just as Kishenji's leadership opened up new possibilities to expand politically, it was under his leadership that they suffered setbacks which dealt a severe blow to the Maoists, with most of its leading members either killed, arrested or forced to surrender. His leadership proved unequal to handle the demands of a movement which was expanding into mass politics but had little time to consolidate. It is here that his strategic and tactical blunders proved fatal. The reckless killings of CPI (M) activists and/or none-too-political attitude towards other political formations working in Jangalmahal were mistakes. But equally in trying to play the CPI (M) against the Trinamool Congress—in Marxist parlance, exploiting division within the ruling classes—the Maoists ended up being exploited by the Trinamool Congress, who then turned against them once they came to power, including executing the cowardly murder of Kishenji. The political naïveté displayed by the Maoists time and again, falling victim to ruling-class machinations and their inability to exploit the contradictions within the ruling-classes is nothing unique. This has been the fate of almost all Communist formations in India who believe that they can exploit ruling-class contradictions whereas it appears that it is the ruling classes who end up exploiting the divisions among the oppressed to their advantage.

What the Maoist leadership failed to realize was that while it had opened up a new vista, the base on which it rested was weak and incapable of sustaining the prominence that they enjoyed in the political arena; organizationally, too, they were weak. Thus even when one applauds Kishenji for demonstrating that open mass politics can be combined with armed struggle, one cannot but also keep in mind that he should be held responsible for the mistakes that brought about its demise. In a manner of speaking, the Maoist movement creates opportunities but is unable to capitalize on them because it has shown itself incapable of sustaining both armed and mass struggle, except as in Dandakaranya.[96]

It is also how this war is conducted which is of foremost importance if we keep in mind that revolutionary war, above all other forms of warfare, is even more of a political project than other forms of warfare; that's because such a war is politics, 'politics of bloodshed', as Mao reminded us. Thus, on 14 January 2013, when the reports first appeared of dead bodies being mutilated and with explosives laid inside them (not stitched, as we were reminded by the spokesperson of CPI-Maoists in the Eastern Zone), it deserves to be critiqued.

The engagement between the security forces of the Indian State and the PLGA soldiers in the forest area of Latehar district, Jharkhand, in January 2013, was an ambush in which the latter cornered a far larger battalion of paramilitary formations and pushed them back, and thereafter things took a vicious turn. The security forces had been on the trail of a senior Maoist leader, a member of the Central Military Commission of the party, for weeks all the way from Gaya-Aurangabad in Bihar to Jharkhand. It was in the course of this chase that the Maoist guerrillas lured the security forces into an ambush and inflicted heavy casualties. Villagers, including women and children, were then forced by the AFU to flank and shield the government soldiers while the combat was on. The villagers were also coerced into fetching the bodies of the dead and injured soldiers when a bomb planted underneath a government soldier exploded, leaving four of the villagers dead. It was then that the PLGA soldiers planted a time bomb in the stomach of a dead soldier which would 'either have exploded at the spot or else when the bodies were being removed'. The statement dated 16 January 2013 and signed by 'Toofan' on behalf of Bihar-Jharkhand, North Chhattisgarh Special Area Military Commission, went on to say that

> if the issue of planting of bomb in a dead body is considered indecent, then even post-mortem should be considered indecent . . . the only reason for PLGA warriors to have planted the bomb in the stomach of a soldier was to cause more damage to the central forces.

The statement concluded by saying that

> in this resistance we are always willing to accept international rules governing war, but when the ruling classes do not adhere to the principles of war then our acceptance or rejection has no meaning. Although Indian ruling classes are bound by international rules our Party is not formally obliged to abide by them.

It is evident that the Indian State wages war against its own people but publicly claims that it is merely 'police action'. The party spokesperson is correct that the Indian government is bound by international norms, in so far as the common Article 3 of the Geneva Conventions 1949 is accepted by them, since India is a signatory to it. It is also true that the Indian State has waged a 'dirty war', be it in the North-East, Jammu and Kashmir or now against the Maoists across nine states, since 'transforming the will and attitude of the people' is its objective. The party's argument gains credence because the Indian government has not only refused to accept that they are engaged in an 'armed conflict' but it has also been guilty of refusing to bring its domestic laws in line with international laws such the Convention against Torture, Enforced Disappearance and Genocide.

So there is little dispute over the role of the Indian State. The contention is over the Maoists' own role. By insisting that when the Indian State refuses to abide by the rules of combat—in such circumstances the nature of resistance is decided by the war imposed by the ruling classes—they miss the moot point. The question is not as the party spokesperson has posed that 'we are not obliged' to follow the Geneva Conventions when the Indian State does not abide by them; the fact is that they themselves are engaged in prosecuting a revolutionary war. Reciprocity is not a principle that applies in revolutionary warfare. Revolutionaries have to be more alert to the need to gain legitimacy in the eyes of the people through their conduct in contrast to the State whose interest is to isolate the rebels from the people (by coercing the people to withdraw support to the rebels) and turn them into non-persons/criminals to deny them legitimacy.

After a successful ambush where the government forces had been pushed back and forced to lift their cordon, there was no pressing military reason for planting a bomb in a dead combatant's body. The rebels had already notched a victory by pushing the AFU to pull back. So why did they decide to cause more damage by using a dead soldier's body to plant explosives? No reason other than 'causing more damage' to the State forces. Instead of a revolutionary project exercising greater influence on their mode of carrying on the war, to allow 'rude acts of mere instinct' only belittles their political objective. And their public statement shows a poor understanding of war as politics. It is as though 'warrior sentiments' were allowed to prevail over other moderating values which Communist revolutionaries must represent.

In an essay, Lenin cautions that:

> the Party . . . can never regard guerilla warfare as the only or even as the chief method of struggle; it means that this method must be subordinated to other

> methods, that it must be commensurate with the chief methods of warfare (regular war), *and must be ennobled by the enlightening and organizing influence of socialism.* And without this latter condition all methods of struggle in bourgeois society brings the proletariat into close association with the various non-proletarian strata above and below it and, if left to the spontaneous course of events become frayed, corrupted and prostituted.[97] [Emphasis added.]

Maoist guerrillas cannot remain oblivious to this.

But what about a situation where their military action appears to make no sense or is read as reckless spilling of blood? For instance, the 27 May attack on Congress leaders on the national highway that links Bastar district with Sukma, is being projected as a 'danger to democracy', to the 'idea of India', and everyone is vying for becoming the most articulate abuser of the Maoists. It is also true that one can raise several questions about the lack of security, lack of road opening partly 'sanitizing' the area and the poor response-time of the security forces who took inordinately long to travel just 10 kilometres from the CRPF camp and the Darbha thana. Also, despite knowing that Mahendra Karma was on the Maoist 'hit list', not only did other senior Congress leaders accompany him but they also did not wonder why a person enjoying 'Z' category protection was so poorly defended. Moreover, while the killing of Mahendra Karma, the leading light of Salwa Judum, can be explained, his role in the forced displacement of 3.54 lakh people from 644 villages and the rape and pillage that SJ represented, can scarcely be forgotten. But loss of other lives is difficult to defend.

Consider the fact that since January 2013, there have been 1015 operations carried out in the Bastar division and that in all these operations, there was no independent observer (unlike fortuitously in the Edesmeta or the

Sarkenguda cases)—one who is privy to what happens—who could tell us about who was picked up or killed, or whether women were attacked sexually. We get to know about this destruction only when news reaches the world outside. But that still leaves unanswered one question: why did they go on to kill the head of the Chhattisgarh Pradesh Congress Committee, Nandkumar Patel, and his son Dinesh after taking them into custody?

But the ambush was not senseless. Eyewitness accounts show that had Maoists wanted, they could have killed many more people in the convoy. But some of the people were provided help with first-aid and given snacks, and were allowed to go and others were stopped by the guerrillas from proceeding towards the spot lest they too came under the crossfire. So why did they kill Nandkumar Patel? I believe this was a deliberate decision to convey the message to the UPA II government and its leaders that they, the Maoists, are ready for a do-or-die battle while the government is hell-bent on crushing them by hook or by crook. There are abundantly clear indications that the government sees war as the way to attract FDI into the lucrative mining sector, and the Congress party has staked its electoral chances in 2014 to defeating the Maoists. By killing Patel, the Maoists' reply is that they see the Congress party as consisting of people who run with the hare and hunt with the hounds, and therefore cannot be trusted.

Thus the killing of Patel and his son, which came just ten days after the Edesmeta massacre by the government forces, is meant to convey that this time they will not play footsie with a ruling-class political formation during elections.

In other words, a targeted and deliberate killing carries a clear political message if we choose to see it, provided we understand war as 'politics of bloodshed'.

# 14
# Other Forms of Resistance

Few social or political activists lead the lives that Maoists/Naxalites do. It is easy to carry on the life of comfort and mouth radicalism just as it is easy to misread passivity for non-violence and preach peace while acquiescing in the wars of suppression launched by the Indian State. To intellectually dismiss that class/caste/religious/gender differences must and can be overcome or that such efforts to overcome them count for nothing is contrary to the real-life experience of those who work consciously and hard to prevail over them. The Maoists have survived. Their existence is a testimony to their achievement of having taken roots among the people. While scholars and activists talk about alternative development models and paradigms, here are Maoists who have been practising it for the last thirty years among millions of Indians. And not only are they developing agriculture, introducing social and economic reforms, debating social mores but are also engaged in working out their own approach to industrialization, mining, etc. It may be a small step when one considers the vast canvas of India. But is there any other political formation that has come anywhere close to working in harmony with nature even as the people progress? What they have achieved against the many odds deserves respect and admiration.

Given this calibre of party membership, would not the Maoists be able to magnify and expand faster were they to work openly? So does it mean that the Maoists are averse to other forms of struggle? It's not as though the party is oblivious to the need to take a leap from the forest strongholds to the plains outside. So the question is: how do they sustain it politically? How can they ensure mass mobilization and mass struggle if they cannot do it on their own steam? It is then one realizes that they either require the helping hand of the radical political formations working openly and legally or to expand through political mobilization under the cover of a broad-based front.

A senior leader drew attention to the fact that when the (Maoist) party mobilized people against feudal landlords in north Telengana of Andhra Pradesh in 1970s and conducted social boycott campaigns against the landlords, military forces were deployed against the party.[98] When the party carried out peaceful anti-liquor campaigns, the police sold arrack and encouraged people to consume alcohol. He recalled that when in the urban areas, colliery workers of Singareni organized themselves under the Singareni Workers Federation in 1981 the union was

> unofficially banned within three years. An undeclared ban was imposed on the students and youth organizations, women's organizations, workers organizations, cultural organizations and every form of peaceful, democratic space available for protest was brutally suppressed . . . it is not the forms of struggle and forms of organization adopted by the party that had led to imposition of ban but the very ban (whether declared or undeclared) on every type of open, legal activity including peaceful public meetings that had compelled the revolutionaries to adopt non-peaceful and armed forms of struggle and underground forms of organization.

Thus, they may not be averse to other forms of struggle but a ban on their overt political activities impinges on their capacity to do so. However, in order to take a leap from the forest strongholds to the plains outside, military victories may be necessary but in themselves remain insufficient, because the question will be to sustain this politically. The fact that the State has criminalized Maoists means that their chances of working openly are severely curtailed. So how can they ensure mass mobilization and mass struggle if they cannot do it on their own? It is then one realizes that they require the aid of the radical political formations working openly and legally. In turn, it means they will have to reconfigure PPW in such a way that what they are unable to do is carried out by other political formations. This would dilute the one-party hegemony.

Besides, as Maoists move closer to relatively developed areas, they will find that the freedoms people fought for and won must be protected. They will have to keep in mind that more than hundred years of struggle have won the Indian working class, rural as well as urban, a variety of freedoms. Much of these freedoms have been legislated, exist on paper, or/and are today under severe attack and devaluation. Yet, if the Maoists have to win over the working people and work with them in areas where they have no or little presence at present, will they not have to work for expanding these freedoms? How do they envisage taking this forward? In other words, they have to politically neutralize the innate hostility that some of these groups entertain about Maoists by offering them space to work in order that they can also be able to carry out the task of mass mobilization where the Maoists cannot work.

What Maoists faced in Jangalmahal was a condition where their political strategy was contested by others from among the pro-people forces. To carry out an armed struggle with acrimonious relations among these forces was difficult and became a problem. In other words, they failed to politically neutralize the innate hostility that some of these groups entertained about the Maoists.

These limitations or obstacles facing them in some areas mean that there is a danger of the Maoists ending up merely playing a *catalytic* role, one of enabling reform of the existing Indian State. They may courageously survive for years inside the jungle strongholds but encirclement can marginalize them materially and intellectually. True, a banned party cannot work openly to mobilize and organize people. War also necessitates that they defend themselves against relentless attacks. The witch-hunt to which they are exposed, the executions carried out by the government forces or arrests of large number of cadres affect their capacity to work, and carry out political education of new recruits. But they compound their problems by antagonizing those working overground among the people. An opportunity was created by them in Jangalmahal where they stood a chance to expand territorially through an armed takeover of the area but even more politically under the cover of a mass organization and an urban solidarity front.

Without cognition of these factors, the Maoists cannot survive outside their forested hill strongholds. Is this a workable proposition? Will this ever happen? Can the ideological fissures be filled?

# Prospects and Problems

If revolutionary warfare is unlike any other form of warfare or seeks to be one by the very nature of what it seeks to achieve, the emancipation of people, then it is how this warfare is understood and conducted that becomes of utmost importance. Recall that partisan war becomes 'a politically charged' term, because, in a revolutionary war

> adherence to a revolutionary party implies nothing less than total integration [Erassung]. Other groups and associations and the state in its current form, are no longer able to integrate their members and adherents so totally as a revolutionary party does its active fighters.[99]

It is this integration that is sought to be achieved and the very process of warfare is linked to ensure this.

The presence of Maoists and their proficiency in armed warfare acts as a check and a counter to the 'savage war for development' that is going on. It is the fear of people joining the Maoist ranks as State repression increases that persuades the State to take reformists *seriously*. The Maoist armed struggle is also a check on the proclivity among the Left parties towards reformism, legalism and electoralism. Above all, the Maoist movement has shown through all its ups and downs that they have the capacity to learn and unlearn, something that has contributed to making them a formidable force, far beyond their actual military prowess.

Thus without the Maoists, the project of revolutionary transformation through seizure of power would not only lose its cutting edge but turn into a distant goal.

Armed struggle plays an emancipatory role when the oppressed are able to defend themselves, when it can save people from being trampled upon by a ruthless military which invariably sides with the rich, the powerful and the privileged. But revolutionary warfare takes it one step higher by imbuing the soldier or the partisan with the revolutionary project to enable seizure of power.

Violence is value neutral. It is how violence is harnessed, for what purpose it is used, that becomes of relevance. To assume that just because fascists use violence and therefore there is no difference between how they use it and how anyone else uses it, or that it is one and the same, is an erroneous assumption. To argue that the death caused by fascists or Maoists is one and the same because the fact is that a person has died, is an argument fraught with contradiction. Those who argue thus must then accept that all deaths caused by the government forces, caste panchayats, immolation of women and what have you, are one and the same because in the end, someone has been killed. By this logic, the death of rioters at the hands of the security forces is one and the same as fake encounters/ custodial killings by the security forces. Or that lynching to death by, say, slum dwellers of a gangster is the same as a caste panchayat carrying out the murder of those who fall in love outside their caste or within the same clan. This is twisted logic. It should matter for the living why deaths take place, to understand the motivation and intent behind them. Thus the political reason behind an act of violence *does matter*. In this sense, getting to know or having an informed view is imperative. Or else it will make inconsequential the difference between extreme right-wing groups for whom a community/ethnic group becomes the enemy and terrorizing civilians is considered perfectly legitimate, and the violence of the left-wing radicals whose focus is on ending the material conditions of oppression of the people in the course of which armed hostilities could ensue. Therefore, we must interrogate how Maoists harness violence for a revolutionary transformation.

Looking strictly in terms of military combat, the Maoist guerrillas are today better trained and have shown adeptness in mobile guerrilla attacks, as exemplified by the looting of armouries, freeing prisoners from jail and causing much embarrassment to the counter-insurgency COBRA units of CRPF, particularly in Chhattisgarh and Jharkhand. Recall the words of the Indian PM on 20 December 2007 at the Chief Ministers' conference on Internal Security

> [n]ot a day passes without an incident of Left Wing Extremism taking place somewhere or the other. Over the last year, the activities of Naxal groups have revealed new aspects. They seem to have developed the *capability* in some areas *to launch frontal attacks* on police forces and establishments. They are certainly targeting all aspects of economic activity. They are *targeting* vital economic infrastructure so as to *cripple* transport and logistic capabilities and also *slow down* any development activity. [Empasis added.]

Some of these have been audacious and fairly large-scale operations such as the ones in Nayagarh, Koraput and Monghyr as well as the Jehanabad and the Dantewada jailbreaks. They involved 200–500 guerrillas travelling over a large territory, preparing for months, taking villagers into confidence, and then disappearing as swiftly as the objective was realized. A recent encounter in Gadchiroli district of Maharashtra showed that 25–30 Maoist guerrillas led by a woman commander held off a 250-strong paramilitary force for ten hours and escaped. With far less ammunition and fewer weapons than the security forces minus the massive logistical backup enjoyed by them to engage in a ten-hour-long exchange of fire reflects on the discipline and training of the guerrillas. At Timliwada of Sukma district in Chhattisgarh recently, the firing by the Maoists on an IAF combat helicopter showed that they have developed indigenous propeller and rocket-launch capabilities.

Even more significant is the fact that the Maoist combat strategy factored in the possibility of aerial warfare against them way back in 2004 and also the need to develop an 'air sentry system'. A document reportedly found by security forces from a Maoist camp asks guerrillas to practise 'concealment' by camouflaging their kit, equipment and tents.[100] It then goes on to guide them on how to use their automatic and semi-automatic rifles: 'To attack a low flying, slow-moving helicopter/plane, aim at a distance of 50 metres (half of a football field) ahead of the plane.' And then says: 'Continuous firing at a definite length in the front of the helicopter will ensure at least that a few rounds will hit sensitive parts like its fuel tank.' At Timliwada, it was the fuel tank that was pierced. So even their most ardent opponents do not deny their shooting skills to defy a huge ensemble of the Armed Forces of the Union. The size of their firepower gets multiplied many times over by the mass support they enjoy in DK. It speaks of their motivation.

But in contrast to the above, there are some operations which stretch the norms of what is acceptable, such as the revenge killing in Jamui, the slaughtering of Francis Induvar and the planting of a time bomb inside a dead combatant's body. In each instance, they had a choice not to overstep the bounds of the acceptable. These were not in any way a military necessity. It may be that such acts terrorize the security forces and those who work for them are gripped by fear. There may even be a short-term generation of popular support as happened in the Latehar district of Jharkhand after the Maoist ambush of government forces. However, in the long run, they also strengthen the resolve of the government personnel, who we know fight not for some 'loftier notions of fighting for the flag and the country' but for battalion honours and out of a sense of loyalty to their fallen comrades.[101] Even in Lalgarh of West Bengal there was some rejoicing by people when the CPM cadres were being punished by the Maoists, including some of them being put to death. However, such rejoicing does not last and erodes as fast as it is generated. So in Lalgarh, the very same killings that once enthused the local population, probably out of a sense of revenge, turned into a divisive factor because they were carried out with such cruelty that it eroded support. To kill a teacher, even one accused of being a tyrant and a crook, in front of his pupils may be found acceptable by some people, but equally it would put off others who will nurse this silently.

Excessive killing or bloodletting always becomes counter-productive and in the long run creates far bigger problems than envisaged. Such is the significance of the Maoist movement in India that any setback suffered by them, politically or militarily, not only impacts on their own cadres but actually influences a much larger radical political formation.

Now it may be that the Indian Maoists reject the Geneva Conventions and Protocols because these are seen as having been worked out by imperialist powers. Although strictly speaking, Soviet Union was as active a participant in formulating the 1949 Geneva Conventions as US or Britain.

So if we consider the Geneva Conventions and Protocols as something dynamic and having evolved out of the sense of horror felt at what transpired during the first and second world wars which helped lay down some protection for civilians and combatants—dead, injured or detained—as well as the dos and don'ts of combat, then the issue becomes entirely different. The Geneva Conventions is not perfect, nor does it address all concerns. The Convention has also been followed in the breach by most member States of the UN. Meanwhile, international criminal law also suffers from the inability to outlaw invasion or aggression, such as the US aggression against Iraq and Afghanistan. What is more, powerful countries such as the US use the *principle of exception* to grant immunity to their military personnel. Thus, the lack of application or non-compliance to these laws by the big powers leaves little incentive for small states as well as rebels/partisans/militants to follow these rules.

Yet, what is forgotten is that the Geneva Conventions and Protocols, by declaring some things as taboo, implicitly also defines what is acceptable military conduct. For instance, a school cannot be targeted by the combatants. However, were the school to be turned into a camp for soldiers, something the Convention argues should not be done, the building then ceases to be a school and becomes acceptable military target. Similarly, informers and couriers in times of war are combatants and their interdiction is not considered wrong (torture, killing are in any case prohibited).

Another consequence of the Conventions is that it helps in generating legitimacy for the rebels/irregulars/partisans. In some cases, it confers legitimacy on rebels when they become formally a party which signs their adherence to the Conventions. But even when rebels do not go through a formal procedure but declare their commitment to abide by them, it becomes an enabling step to earn legitimacy. Nation-states have a propensity to demonize and criminalize rebels precisely to protect the status quo, whereas the rebels/revolutionaries have to fight the heavy odds arrayed against them by seizing opportunities available which can help them gain legitimacy. In other words, the Convention is politically relevant for them as it protects their own self-interest.

So the Geneva Conventions remain the cornerstone of contemporary international criminal law. It contains the essential rules protecting persons who are not or no longer taking a direct part in hostilities or when they find themselves in the hands of an adverse party. The Conventions may not be adequate, and the Indian State may be reluctant to adhere to it out of fear of its military personnel getting prosecuted and/or earning opprobrium because their combat conduct is patently savage. So, what the Geneva Conventions do is to set some benchmark for combatants to adhere to. For instance, the

> 1977 Additional Protocols were drawn up essentially as a response to changes in warfare, most notably the expansion of guerrilla warfare, and the increased suffering of civilians in armed conflict due in part to developments in weapons technology. *They introduced essential rules relating to the conduct of hostilities and the methods and means of warfare, the aim of which was to strengthen protection for civilians. In particular, they formulated the important principle of distinction between civilians and combatants and between civilian objects and military objectives.* They have also expanded the list of fundamental guarantees applicable to all persons in the power of an adverse party.[102] [Emphasis added.]

It is worth stressing that the civilian–combatant divide of the Conventions is not the same as the argument that people are 'sandwiched' between the warring combatants. The divide is to ensure a difference between civilian and military objectives or targets, and to lay down minimum norms for combat. Thus, even when people support Maoists they cannot be targeted by the government forces, precisely because those not armed are prohibited from being harmed. For some to invoke civilian-combatant difference to espouse their propaganda that people are being 'squeezed' between two warring sides is nothing but conflating people with civilians, whereas people is a political construct representing those oppressed and exploited by the ruling classes. Some of them can be armed and others need not be.

Nevertheless, for the revolutionaries there is a need to invest their People's War with values which distinguishes their conduct, especially in combat, from that of the government forces.

Arguably, if a revolutionary war is for seizure of power, then stopping short of total or absolute war (military victory) may appear to run counter to what the revolutionaries desire or perceive to be imperative. However, revolutionaries cannot remain impervious to change or to modification of their strategy in line with circumstances and possibilities where militarily overwhelming the ruling classes appear difficult to realize. There is, in other words, nothing pre-ordained that only military victory will pave the way for takeover of power. In other words, class war based on *absolute enmity* does not automatically mean going in for total war. When other options are either available or can emerge in the course of the fighting, what brings about a closure and how the military showing on the ground is leveraged to bring this about, are all possibilities which can never be ruled out.

Engels, Lenin and Mao, all three weighed war differently. Engels, troubled by possibilities of an all-out war in Europe grew wary; Lenin, who saw possibilities for Russia in the war, was not unaware of its pitfalls; whereas Mao because of the context within which the Chinese revolution was unfolding was the most enthusiastic votary of military seizure of power. All of them took war seriously and made it a point to analyse developing situations; as a result, even when they refused to reject the importance of war, they let the concrete reality and where they were placed, to appreciate or depreciate its importance. Where war is deprecated as a matter of some a priori fundamental norm, the critical significance of war gets muscled out, so much so that we fail to even take note of the spin-offs of war, not all of which are negative. This also comes in the way of realizing that revolutionary warfare is altogether different.

Furthermore, to fight or not to fight the class war—and if it has to be fought, to fight it by investing it with values—is one aspect of revolutionary warfare. But there are other aspects as well that have to be kept in mind. In war, as in politics, choosing strategic friends and allies as well as fighting the main enemy is of decisive significance. Carl Schmitt points out that

> [w]ar finds its meaning in enmity. Because it is continuation of politics, politics too always involves an element of enmity, at least potentially; and if peace contains within itself the possibility of war—something that by the standards of experience has unfortunately proved to be true—peace too contains a moment of potential enmity.[103]

The question, however, is whether the enmity can be contained and regulated, that is, whether it represents 'relative or absolute enmity'. To treat as an enemy an ideological opponent while enhancing the importance of a tactical ally in the shape of a ruling-class formation is to devalue and obviate the distinction between friend and enemy and between strategic and tactical friends. Revolutionary warfare is also not based on the principle of reciprocity.

While war is the continuation of politics by other means, Mao also pointed out that 'war is politics with bloodshed'. Meaning thereby that the practice of warfare is part of the political. But the political distinguishes itself not by enmity, which war does. As Carl Schmitt says the 'heart of political is not enmity per se but the distinction of friends and enemy'.[104] For instance, to treat as enemy an ideological/ political opponent while enhancing the importance of the tactical ally in the shape of a ruling-class formation, is a dilution of revolutionary politics, which is based on absolute enmity. This warfare also combines mass struggle with armed struggle. One without the other makes revolutionary warfare redundant. So in 'learning by doing' it is important not to forget that the 'war' being waged cannot be prosecuted by placing military needs ahead of other requirements. In Jangalmahal, for instance, the needs of war were used to justify the indiscriminate killing of 'informers'; above all, controlling the mass front, PCAPA, and then going public with it, weakened the rebels just when a united mass struggle was what was most needed.

Dividing the enemy is tactically useful but keeping your allies, real as well as potential, with you is even more important. PCAPA was a coalition of class friends and allies. There were others who were earlier part of the struggle but had parted ways. Many were political opponents but were certainly part of the broad coalition with a pro-revolutionary bent. By pushing them out and/or to resolve political battles through annihilation weakened the mass movement. Instead of helping their war efforts, it actually brought about its debilitation. Thus Bernard De'Mello draws attention to the fact that

> [w]hat makes the implementation of massline even more difficult is Article 59 of the Constitution of the Party that directs the Party fraction in the mass organization to dictate terms thereby encouraging 'commandism' which can lead to 'isolationism', i.e., the Party ultimately failing to gain the support of the non-Party leaders of its mass organizations.[105]

The examples cited elsewhere are meant to reveal the fallout of *partial mobilization* by the Maoists, against the background of divisions among the oppressed classes, often at odds over common property. Working to impose the party's own domination over mass movements, more often than not, weakens mass struggles. These are throwing up contradictions which if not addressed could gravely harm the revolutionary movement. While accepting the legitimacy of armed struggle, we ought to be clear that this does not mean a carte blanche for brutish and cruel conduct. We do distinguish between deaths. We mourn the death of our heroes but will not mourn for tyrants. We mourn when civilians get killed but not when murderous gangs are wiped out. When actual encounters take place and combatants on either side get killed we do not condemn it; we at best lament the loss of lives due to a war foisted on the people by the government. We distinguish between killing and killing by recourse to cruel methods. The war, for the revolutionaries, is not a celebration of bloodletting (as was common in the early phase of the Naxalbari movement where killing of the 'class enemy' was glorified). These differences are grounded in political ethics. To be firm in resolve, for example, is not the same as being unmindful of committing excesses.

It is true that Clausewitz, unlike Lenin or Mao, considered 'absolute war' as fantasy because politics and society impose constraints, whereas absolute war throws up the possibility of a war to the finish. The goal of a purely military victory is a part of PPW, although Maoists insist that politics even then does not get subordinated to the goal of military victory. So the first aspect is that the inability to carve out a 'liberated zone', an area where revolutionaries are in control, shows that in the twenty-first century the notion of military victory by revolutionary forces may no longer be relevant and it is possible to think in terms of containment and regulation of war without giving up absolute enmity, which is necessary for the overthrow of the State and its substitution by a new socialist democracy.

The experience of Maoists in Nepal has thrown up this possibility. However, to be fair, the path chosen by them has so far manifested poor results and instead resulted in a split. But is it possible to envisage the possibility of a military stalemate forcing the pace for a negotiated democratic closure? Although the Maoists in Nepal failed, India is far more advanced in socio-economic and political terms. Should this not be taken into account?

It is worth recalling that in India, the PPW is taking place in a situation where both 'politics without bloodshed' as well as 'politics with bloodshed' are present side by side and at times overlap. Political plurality in India also means a different history and contestation within the Indian Left with multiple Communist formations, parliamentary to extra-parliamentary parties, six-decade-long multiparty system, presence of a large middle class, funded or non-funded activism, and above all the country's multi-national and multi-ethnic lived culture. The Maoists have shown the capacity to negotiate themselves through this and the continuing support they get from the most oppressed classes illustrates this. But it is worth remembering that it is easy to divide people when class differentiations are not sharp, and caste/ religious/ethnic divisions can easily be stoked. When this is combined with moments of elation such as when a corrupt party is removed from power through elections or when the government bows down to pressure to pass a law or modify a draconian law, or a judgment questions the notion of 'guilt by association', rejects charge of sedition, upholds people's right to land . . . all these show that a concerted popular campaign can succeed. Saner voices in the judiciary, bureaucracy and political leadership, do at times prevail. It creates the impression that it is possible to get things done within the parameters of the prevailing system. But this also provides the Indian State the resilience to ride roughshod over dissent and popular discontent, and to emerge out of it intact. This necessitates paying careful attention to how to distinguish between friends and enemies, and wage a mass struggle.

Comparing the Russian and Chinese revolutions, Issac Deutscher perceptively pointed out that

> [i]n Russia the civil war was waged after the revolution, whereas in China it had been fought before the revolution. The question of whether communists enter the civil war as a ruling party or as a party of opposition is of the greatest consequence for their subsequent relationship with all classes of society.

And then goes on to say that:

> The establishment of the single party system in China was not the painful and dramatic crisis it had been in Russia, for the Chinese had never had the taste of any genuine multiparty system. No Social Democratic reformism had struck roots in Chinese

> soil. Maoism has never had to contend with opponents as influential as those that had defied Bolshevism: there were no Chinese Mensheviks or Social Revolutionaries . . . Maoism was never in the throes of a deep conflict with its own past, such as troubled the Bolshevik mind when it was being forced into the monolithic mould.[106]

The absence of political democracy in China, or at least its weak foundation, is a strong argument against adopting the same strategy in contemporary India with its political plurality and an altogether different historical context. The extent to which bourgeoisie democracy has taken roots in India then must be factored in to modify the notion of 'absolute war', i.e., a military seizure of power. This was the challenge posed to the Nepalese Maoists and they chose to engage with this rather than carry on with their PPW. Somewhere they were questioning the idea of a clinching military victory.

But did the Nepalese Maoists seriously err where 'absolute enmity' was concerned? Did they vacillate when parties of the status quo did everything possible to isolate and marginalize them by taking over power in April 2006 when the Maoists were kept out from the interim coalition government and again after they emerged as the largest party in the elections to the Constituent Assembly in 2009 and were denied the opportunity to form the government? Did they make major concessions by giving up one after another their major strategic assets in the form of their social and political reforms? There are also reasons to believe that the leadership of Prachanda-Bhattarai mistook military stalemate as a mark of their own weakness, forgetting the axiom that in an insurgency a situation of stalemate means political setback for the government forces and advantage for the guerrillas because the State forces are unable to defeat them. The rights and wrongs of this phase in Nepal and subsequent retreats are still a subject matter of dispute within Nepal's Maoist party which stands split. But what lessons do we learn from their self-inflicted setback? The probability is that the Maoists in India will settle for military capture of power. However, there is a need to take a critical look at Nepal's experience if only to analyse what prospects got opened up, if any, and where they botched the opportunities that came their way.

In conditions that apply in India—where one-party hegemony is difficult to envisage considering the diversity and political plurality with which we have lived for more than a hundred years–to believe that the Maoists can inspire others to merge their identity by becoming part of the Maoists appears a distant possibility. The tension between a hegemonic project and fragmented and partial mobilization in reality will not end any time soon. Nevertheless, without armed struggle, social transformation of the Indian State and society too is inconceivable. Also, it would be political naiveté to completely rule out the need for an urban strategy. Because no matter how politically conscious Indians are, or are not for that matter, it is the concrete reality, always in a state of flux, that matters. Just as the Indian State has exhibited utter contempt for its own laws and the Constitution, ensuring that State functionaries are cocooned through legal 'exception' when and where it suits them, there is absolutely nothing to say that circumstances cannot bring about a situation where people are left with no choice but to defend themselves and the freedoms that they won through struggle. Thus, there is nothing absolutely given or fixed. What appears difficult to imagine today may become a dire necessity tomorrow. The question, however, is whether the pursuit of a method to bring about seizure of power remains immutable or is in need of change invested with progressive and emancipatory values.

To sum up, what is important to remember is that it is the presence of the Maoist armed struggle that creates space for unarmed mass protests to sprout and take root. In this sense, it is impossible to separate one from the other—both provide the condition for the other to become strong.

Class war compels that the revolutionaries, through their own practice, mark out their difference from the reactionary classes. They must fight their battles honourably, keeping in mind the need to mobilize the masses and to inspire them to organize themselves. To believe that niceties of ethical warfare or Geneva Conventions and Protocols are but an attempt to emasculate class war—if not to tie them down with too many principles, especially when the ruling classes carry out a 'dirty war'—is to ignore that the politics of revolutionary warfare is to win over the largest numbers of people, supported by armed cadres for seizure of power. Winning popular legitimacy for their armed struggle not only pushes the political to the forefront, it enables resistance to focus attention on the 'dirty war' prosecuted by the State as well as make the Maoist party realize that it is not infallible and it needs to make corrections. If some practices in the conduct of PPW are acting as impediments to that objective, then it calls for a fresh look at the strategy and tactics of revolutionary warfare in the specific conditions that operate in India. Because the simple truth is that without the Maoists, the project of revolutionary transformation of India cannot be realized.

# Conclusion

Apart from the prudery displayed by Marxists regarding war and its significance, there is another form of prudery that opposes war in the name of opposing 'political violence' while grossly underplaying structural violence. In accepting the legitimacy of the State enjoying 'monopoly' over the means of violence, what is forgotten is that when the State seeks to use this monopoly to push policies and promote the politics of benefitting private and foreign capital, then it is simply naïve to believe that everyone either must or will submit to this diktat meekly. It will be resisted and resistance will express itself in multiple ways depending on the nature of the State's response. The ablest and the most sensitive Indian bemoans violence and condemns it but has rarely been able to muster courage to come out on the street and protest wars against people or against the crimes being committed by the Armed Forces of the Union. What they oppose is the violence employed by people for their self-preservation. But violence that causes millions of lives to remain short, brutal and without dignity and liberty, somehow escapes this moral compass.

In contrast, when we analyse and understand the PPW of the Maoists, it brings out certain salient features of the revolutionary war. We learn how it has progressed, its shortcomings which point to what stymies their expansion, how important their warfare is for freeing people from the double yoke of exploitation and oppression. The simple truth is that it was the Maoist PPW that had stalled the plans of the establishment from opening up forest areas such as Saranda in Jharkhand, to the mining and other industrial interests. This was driven home most effectively when the Maoist withdrawal from Saranda forest saw the government first set up seventeen camps of Central Paramilitary Forces there followed by the Forest Advisory Council beginning the process of clearing proposals from the mining conglomerates. All those who waxed eloquent about the power of non-violent protests went into hibernation while the forests were being opened up for mineral extraction. This development itself lends credibility to the Maoists and silences their critics who condemn them for their PPW.

This itself brings out the importance of taking wars seriously. Carl Schmitt emphasizes:

> Martial theory has to do with discrimination of enmity, which gives war its meaning and character. Every attempt at containing or fencing in war must involve the consideration that in relation to the concept of war enmity is the primary concept, and that the distinction between various kinds of war is preceded by the discrimination among various kinds of enmity.[107]

Thus, politics distinguishes itself by differentiating between friends and enemies whereas wars require discriminating between different types of enmity. Which is to say that even when wars are continuation of politics by other means, wars have a specificity which cannot be ignored.

What I have tried to show is the imperative need to take wars seriously—to understand why wars are waged against people as well as why people take up arms to defend themselves. To regard wars to be abhorrent does not mean that we close our eyes to the reality of wars. Of course, in choosing the Maoist PPW, I was choosing the best or the highest form of warfare to draw attention to the need to take wars seriously. So what about other wars?

Take Afghanistan, for instance. There are some who believe that the developments in Afghanistan show that all talk of ethics and morality of war, Taliban's political ideology, etc., is of no consequence because the important thing is Taliban remain a strong fighting force. I am not so convinced. The fear aroused over the Taliban takeover and the resultant fissures do not augur well for them. Because, whatever battles they win could get blunted by internal divisions (easy fodder for external actors), which will turn the sweet taste of victory very bitter. Thus, it is not about how many battles one wins; what counts is whether after victory, they are able to sustain their control. This is why it is politics that matters. How do they ensure that 50 per cent of the population—women—do not get enslaved and Afghanistan's other ethnic communities do not feel alienated from power? How do they ensure that neighbouring countries and big powers do not feel threatened? Finally, how do they ensure that the region wins some respite from nearly four decades of imperialist-fomented wars?

However, it cannot be denied that Taliban's military resilience has lent them legitimacy; the world believed they had lost after 11 September 2001. It is remarkable that within twelve years of '9/11' when it was being said that war as an option for popular movements was a thing of the past, it has made a comeback. So wars are neither unattractive nor becoming unattractive. The frequency and number of wars being waged by nation-states as well as wars of aggression and proxy wars by big powers show an increase. Far more significantly, wars do force change and win legitimacy. So we cannot deny that winning legitimacy and the politics that command the war remains a key, if not a decisive and desired, factor.

Closer home in Jammu and Kashmir, armed militancy has played the most significant role in empowering a people living under military occupation. For a people considered non-martial-like, militancy armed the ordinary Kashmiri men and women with confidence and courage. Only this can explain the mass upsurge of 2008–10 and the emergence of stone-pelters, courageous youth who faced bullets with stones and despite crackdown, torture and criminal cases, refused to be cowed down. So how wars empower the people suffering military suppression and inspire them to carry on is something that is little realized.

Just as by interrogating wars, we are also provided an important source of understanding the social reality of what it does to the State and its institutions and the impact it has on the people. Let me conclude by quoting Lenin who, writing on 'Principles of Socialism and the War of 1914–15', says:

> Socialists have always condemned war between nations as barbarous and brutal. But our attitude towards war is fundamentally different from that of the bourgeois pacifists (supporters and advocates of peace) and of the Anarchists. We differ from the former in that we understand the inevitable connection between wars and the class struggle within the country; we understand that war cannot be abolished unless classes are abolished and Socialism is created; and we also differ in that we fully regard civil wars, i.e., wars waged by the oppressed class against the oppressing class, slaves against slave-owners, serfs against land-owners, and wage-workers against the bourgeoisie, as legitimate, progressive and necessary. We Marxists

> differ from both the pacifists and the Anarchists in that we deem it necessary historically (from the standpoint of Marx's dialectical materialism) to study each war separately. In history there have been numerous wars which, in spite of all the horrors, atrocities, distress and suffering that inevitably accompany all wars, were progressive, i.e., benefited the development of mankind by helping to destroy the exceptionally harmful and reactionary institutions (for example, autocracy or serfdom), the most barbarous despotisms in Europe (Turkish and Russian). Therefore, it is necessary to examine the historically specific features of precisely the present war.[108]

This was relevant for Russia in early twentieth century and remains relevant for contemporary India because it is the Indian State that has shown a propensity to wage savage wars against the people, whereas the Adivasis led by the Maoists are waging a war for their self-preservation.

# Acknowledgements

My interest in the subject of revolutionary warfare was triggered off by my conversations with Jan Myrdal. This began when, together with him, I met senior leaders of the CPI (Maoist) in January 2010 where I had raised the issue of CPI (Maoist) accepting the public appeal of the Indian civil liberties movement to adhere to Geneva Conventions and its Protocol II. This finds reference in his book (*Red Star over India: As the Wretched of the Earth are Rising*; Kolkata: Setu Prakashani, 2012; pp. 118–24). The conversation between me and Jan Myrdal carried on thereafter where he drew my attention to the history of the Geneva Conventions and it was thanks to him that I was able to access some of the material available in English on the question of partisans/irregulars and how they became de-criminalized as belligerents, the difference between 'absolute' versus the 'real' war, which could be contained and regulated, the evolution of Geneva Conventions, how Prussia violated every tenet of the Geneva Conventions during the war against the Paris Commune or how the Versailles regime massacred more than 70,000 Parisians while the Paris Commune killed 70, and yet it is the latter which is vilified and not the former, just as in our own times bigger warmongers and war criminals, namely US-led NATO, escape prosecution for crimes against humanity while leaders of smaller African or Balkan states are brought to justice. It is also astonishing that there are sparse English translations of some of the literature on this subject in other European languages. This silence tells its own story of how perception can be and is managed even within broadly Left, English-speaking segment of the world. I am also obligated to Bernard D'Mello, for his incisive comments and for drawing my attention to several issues of *Socialist Register* which critiqued Maoism. Some of my preliminary writings appeared in *Sanhati* and *Frontier*. I am thankful to them for enabling me to reach out to a wider audience. My colleagues in PUDR will recognize that some of the issues arise from our own attempts to grapple with them. Just as Sahba will recognize our own discussions and differences that has helped me along. Parvez, Khurram, Zahir and Kartik and scores of others in Kashmir helped remove 'nationalist' cobwebs and clear my conception of armed conflict/war in a very fundamental way. But none of this would have meant much without Alpa Shah's exhortation that I write this down for a conference she was organizing. Her sharp comments on an earlier draft helped me more than she realizes. I have been fortunate in having Shanuj Cheruvakodan read the draft. Bringing 'shine' to a dark and dense draft requires a lot of doing. I cannot thank him enough. I am grateful to Ankita Anand for her help with copy-editing. The comfort level I enjoy with her enables me to work without feeling stressed or troubled.

But all my efforts and all the help rendered by so many people would have come to nought had it not been for the persistence of Subrata who approached me to write this book for Setu Prakashani. His patience and perseverance played a very important role. However, the contents and arguments which follow are mine alone.

## *Endnotes*

1. *Small Wars; Their Principles & Practice*: Colonel C.E. Callwell; Third Edition, University of Nebraska Lincoln and London 1996, p. 26.
2. *Indian Express*, 8 February 2013. On 17 May 2013 the *Times of India* reported that Cabinet Committee on Infrastructure has cleared two proposals, a third proposal for mining will be cleared. Meanwhile the Jharkhand state government has prepared a list of 155 mines it wants opened up in the 800 sq kms of Saranda forest. Newspapers reported that while the forest is an 'ecologically sensitive zone', the 'overall economic growth of state and the country' requires this opening of the forest for mining.
3. *The Theory of the Partisan: A Commentary/Remark on the Concept of the Political*; Carl Schmitt; Michigan University Press, 2004, p. 64. There were several features of the Spanish war (1808-14) that drew Europe's attention. For one the Spanish army 'ill-equipped and sketchily supported' and their 'ranks filled with untrained recruits' suffered heavy losses but were 'not destroyed'. The same Spanish army which was no match for French army would return to 'plague' the French army. Thus three-fourths of the French army remained unavailable to meet the British forces led by Wellington as these guerrillas kept harassing the far superior French troops. For another it was a regular army which was an ill-match for Napoleon's troops turned irregular and inflicted much damage and kept the French forces tied down. Marx writing on Guerilla Warfare, which refers to Spain's war against France, (1808–14) quotes approvingly. 'It was,' says the Abbé de Pradt, 'neither battles nor engagements which exhausted the French forces, but the incessant molestations of an invisible enemy, who, if pursued, became lost among the people, out of which he reappeared immediately afterward with renewed strength. The lion in the fable tormented to death by a gnat gives a true picture of the French army.' http://www.marxists.org /archive/marx/works/1854/revolutionary-spain/ch05.htm.

Thus the Spanish War of Independence had. It is this that caught the imagination of many young military officers in Europe, one of them being Clausewitz. For more read 'Origins of Guerilla Doctrine', Journal of Contemporary History, Walter Laquer, July 1975 10: pp. 341–82.

4. On 31 December 2006 the chief of Army Staff general J.J. Singh released the '*Doctrine for Sub Conventional Operations*' brought out by the 'Integrated Headquarters in the Ministry of Defense (Army)'. www.indianarmy.nic.in/indar_doctrine.htm; p. 1.
5. Consider the fact that India's Ministry of Home Affairs has said that they oppose repatriation of 50 per cent of the Pakistani convicts who have served their sentence arguing that such spies and terrorists could pose a threat to India's security! See *Hindustan Times*, 14 May 2013.
6. *A Matter of Honour: An Account of the Indian Army, Its Officers and Men*: Philip Mason; EBD Educational Pvt Ltd, Dehradun 1988; p. 531. See also pp. 13–17.
7. *History of Warfare*; John Keegan; Vintage Books, New York 1994; p. 1.
8. Ibid; pp. 391–92.
9. *New and Old Wars: Organised Violence in a Global Era*; Mary Kaldor; Polity Press, Cambridge (UK) 2012; p. 215.
10. Luke Mogelson writing in *New York Times* Magazine on 17 January 2013 on the war in Afghanistan.
11. See Criminal Appeal No. 257 of 2011 General Officer Commanding versus CBI and Anr. With Criminal Appeal No. 55 of 2006 Additional Director General vs CBI, in short Pathribal judgment. And Criminal Appeal No. 624 of 2013 [SLP(CRL) No. 5910 of 2012] State of J&K versus Lakhwinder Kumar & Ors with Criminal Appeal No. 625 of 2013 [SLP(CRL) No. 5911 of 2012] Ghulam Mohammed Sheikh versus State of J&K and Ors, in short Zahid Sheikh case.
12. See *Alleged Perpetrators: Stories of Impunity in Jammu and Kashmir*; International People's Tribunal for Human Rights and Justice in Indian Administered Kashmir and Association of Parents of Disappeared Persons, Srinagar 2012; www.kashmirprocess.org. This is the first study in India which has broken the cover of anonymity which protects the perpetrators by raising the principle of 'individual criminal responsibility'. Equally it raises the principle of Command Responsibility and principle of Joint Criminal Enterprise all of which forms part of International

Criminal Law. The Indian State 'authorizations' to armed forces to carry out every kind of operation, often without adherence to laws and norms under draconian legislations such as AFSPA on the pretext of combating militant violence while simultaneously being in breach of bringing India's domestic laws in line with International Conventions such as against Torture, Enforced Disappearance and Genocide compounds the impunity extended to India's security forces because certain crimes are non-justiciable under Indian's domestic law. It refutes the claim of the Indian state that commission of crimes is an aberration rather than a policy. It indicts the Indian State for pursuing a policy which engenders the state of impunity by listing 500 individual perpetrators, which include 235 army personnel, 123 paramilitary personnel, 111 Jammu and Kashmir Police personnel and 31 government backed militants/associates. It shows how State violence is institutionalized through a culture of institutional impunity to the State forces where the police, the judiciary and other organs of the government perpetuate the state of human rights violation.

13. 'I see mothers with children, I see fathers with children, I see fathers with mothers. I see kids playing soccer', said Col. D. Scott Brenton of the US air force sitting in Syracuse fighting a war in Afghanistan and then firing missiles while the hair on his neck stood up but stating, 'I feel no emotional attachment to the enemy . . . I have a duty and I execute the duty.' *Indian Express* reprint of an article from *New York Times* filed by Elisabeth Bumiller, 31 July 2012.
14. *Hindustan Times* (Delhi edition) 10 November 2012.
15. *Class Struggles in France: 1848–1850*; Karl Marx with an introduction by Frederik Engels; SW Vol I, Progress Publishers, Moscow 1973; p.198.
16. Ibid.
17. *Philosophers of War and Peace: Kant, Clausewitz, Marx, Engels and Tolstoy*; K.B. Galle; Cambridge University Press; p. 67.
18. Engels from his letter to Babel (1882). Loc. Cit. in Galle, ibid. p. 92.
19. International Socialism Journal Winter 2002; Issue 97, Gilbert Achcar.
20. Schmitt, Carl. Ibid; p. 35. Real War 'is a wonderful trinity, composed of the original violence of its elements, of the play of probabilities and chance which make it a free activity of the soul, and of its subordinate nature as a political instrument, in which respect it belongs to the province of Reason . . .' Clausewitz cited by Galle, ibid, pp. 49– 50. Lenin in 'The Military Programme of the

Proletarian Revolution' also reminds us that 'national wars under imperialism' as well as 'civil wars, which in every class society are the natural, and under certain conditions inevitable' cannot be denied. Lenin also offered the thesis of advancing the socialist cause by using the opportunity offered by the 'capitalist war'. Much of contemporary social life continues to be and will continue to be dictated/influenced/caused by war/s, whether it takes shape of Afghan Resistance against US-NATO invasion or civil war to overthrow a military dictatorship or to overthrow oppressive class rule or a popular resistance against national tyranny as the Palestinian struggle against Israel etc. or class wars such as the PPW of CPI (Maoist).

21. Mao Ze Dong; On Protracted War; May 1938. http://www.marxists.org/refernce/archive/mao/selected-works/volume
22. V.I. Lenin: *Bellicose Militarism & the Anti-Militarist Tactics of Social Democrats (1908); Volume 15; pp. 191–201.*
23. Ibid.
24. Leon Trotsky: *Notes on War*: A collection of sixty articles reprinted from the Pall Mall www.marxists.org/archive/trotsky/1924/03/english.html.
25. V.I. Lenin: Guerilla Warfare (1906); Volume 11; pp. 213–23.
26. Loc. Cit. in Carl Schmitt, p. 42.
27. *Guerilla Warfare*: Authorized edition with corrections made by Che Guevara. Leftword, Delhi 2012, p. 75.
28. Galle, ibid., p. 75.
29. Mao Tse Tung 'On Guerilla Warfare' www.Marxists.org/reference/archive/mao/works/1937/guerilla.
30. Ibid.
31. Schmitt, ibid., p. 10.
32. Mao Tse Tung, On Protracted War; May 1938. marxists.org/reference/archive/mao/selected-works/volume-2/mswv2_09.htm.
33. Ibid.
34. Ibid.
35. Sebastian Junger, *War*, Fourth Estate, London 2011 p. 33.
36. *The Statesman*, 23 November 2012.
37. *Times of India*, 2 November 2012.
38. *Times of India*, 7 October, 2010.

39. Loc. Cit. in *The Week* where a former member of DK Special Zonal Committee of CPI (Maoist Raghu Sadmate was interviewed after his surrender, in police custody, by the magazine (12 May 2013) was asked 'Are the allegations of female cadres being sexually exploited by comrades and commanders true? Are married couple not allowed to have children?' He answered, 'No. That is wrong. Nobody is allowed to sexually exploit female cadres. Anybody doing that will be killed. Every dalam has four or five female cadres. They, too, have weapons. Women are about 45 per cent of the total strength of the Maoists. Yes, if they marry among themselves, they are not allowed to have children because the attachment can affect their work as Maoists. But now, I hear a few have children.'
40. *Tehelka*; Volume 7, Issue 18, 8 May 2010.
41. Sudhir Kakar, *A Book of Memory: Confessions and Reflections*, Penguin-Viking, Delhi 2011, p. 281.
42. Politics of Violence, Uday Mehta in *Democratic Culture: Historical and Philosophical Essays, edited by Akeel Bilgrami*; Routledge, Taylor and Davis Group; New Delhi 2010.
43. Ibid., p. 108.
44. Ibid., p. 113.
45. The Terror of Law: UAPA and the Myth of National Security; Coordination of Democratic Rights Organisation; April 2012, pp. 82–84.
46. Randhir Singh, *Marxism, Socialism, Indian Politics: A View from the Left*, Aakar Books, New Delhi 2008; p. 327.
47. Ibid. pp. 328–47.
48. Dr Binayak Sen pointed out, delivering the sixth IG Khan Memorial Lecture on 'Violence and Justice in Our Times' at Aligarh Muslim University (AMU) on Saturday, 13 March 2010, that the action against Maoists is only accentuating the problem of malnutrition in tribal areas. According to him malnutrition should be the most pressing concern of the government. Military campaign against Maoists and displacement of tribals, he underlined, would only make things worse. 'The government is displacing a large number of people from the very resource base that they are surviving on. Use of words like collateral damage by the government is dangerous as the Maoists don't carry a label on their head.' A person with a body mass index of less than 18.5 is malnourished. According to the National Nutrition Monitoring Bureau, 33 per cent of adult Indians have a BMI of less than 18.5. If

you disaggregate this, over 50 per cent Scheduled Tribes, 60 per cent of the Schedule Castes and an equally high percentage of Muslims have a BMI of 18.5 or are undernourished. He went on to say that '[t]he WHO says that any community of which over 40 per cent population has a BMI of 18.5 per cent is in a state of famine. By that standard, many communities in India are living in a state of famine. Orissa, whose 40 per cent population is undernourished, too, fits the bill.'

He also stated on 3 May 2010 while speaking to students of Asian College of Journalism in Chennai that '[m]ost people think that genocide has to do with large scale direct killing, but the declaration of the Convention on Prevention and Punishment of the Crimes of Genocide, which was issued on 9 December 1948, one day before Universal Declaration of Human Rights, tells us clearly that in addition to killing, the creation of 'physical and mentally hazardous conditions' which could put the survival of particular communities at risk 'would also come within the ambit of genocide'. What is shocking is the inability of our leadership to read the writing on the wall . . .' [Its Article 2 defines genocide as 'any of the following acts committed with intent to destroy, in whole or in part, a national, ethnical, racial or religious group, as such: killing members of the group; causing serious bodily or mental harm to members of the group; deliberately inflicting on the group conditions of life, calculated to bring about its physical destruction in whole or in part; imposing measures intended to prevent births within the group; [and] forcibly transferring children of the group to another group.']

49. Planning Commission in its report prepared by an Expert Group titled *Development Challenges in Extremist Affected Area,* July 2008.
50. Doctrine of Sub conventional Operations; ibid.
51. Ibid.
52. Ibid.
53. Ibid.
54. In December 2006 the US army released its own 282 page long Manual on 'Counter Insurgency': Head Quarters, Department of the Army, December 2006. www.fas.org/irp/doddir/army/fm3-24.pdf. The coincidence of the two being released so close to each other is interesting. The Foreword comes straight to the point and says that 'all insurgencies even today's highly adaptable strains remains 'wars amongst the people' (p. 2). In this war the success of Counter-Insurgency (COIN) depends on 'the people

taking charge of their own affair and consenting to the government rule. Achieving this condition requires the government to eliminate as many causes of the insurgency as feasible. This can include eliminating those extremists whose beliefs prevent them from ever reconciling with the government' (p. 13). In other words it means 'population control' which 'includes determining who lives in an area and what they do . . . Establishment control normally begins with conducting a census and issuing identification cards'. Other measures to control the population includes: 'curfew; a pass system; limits on lengths of time people can travel limits on number of visitors from outside the area with a requirement to register them with local security forces or civil authorities; check posts along major routes and enforce compliance with population control measures' (p. 123). In another place without any sense of irony they say that 'insurgents are constrained by neither the law nor the bonds of human decency as Western nations understand them'(1-160, p. 40). And is quite blasé at another place where it says that 'after security has been achieved, dollars and ballots will have more important effects than bombs and bullets' and when 'money is ammunition' (1-153, p. 39). An obvious difference between the Indian and the US approaches is that the US manual deals with COIN theatre as being outside the borders of the US whereas for India it is related to their operation within the constitutionally ordained borders. This maybe the reason that US COIN includes air bombings, missile attacks, helicopter gunships, navy war ships, etc., since it not at home but abroad whereas in India the approach is of heavy deployment of troops on the ground with 'area domination' as the purpose. This may account for the higher casualties in Iraq between March 2003 to December 2006 of 150-6,00,000 people who died as against the more than two decades of year death count of more than 70,000 in J&K. But whatever be the approach both acknowledge that the hostile are from 'amongst the people'. Both use means brutal and benign, fair and foul to bring about their surrender or their liquidation. And both want to coerce the people to realize the futility of fighting them.

55. Ibid.
56. Doctrine. Ibid.
57. US COIN. Ibid.
58. Ibid.
59. Ibid.

60. Ibid., p. 2.
61. Ibid., p. 13.
62. Ibid., p. 123.
63. Ibid., p. 40.
64. Ibid., p. 39.
65. *Evolving Medical Strategies for Low Intensity Conflict: A Necessity;* Lt Col Ajay Dheer, Lt Col Jaipuria, Col HK Sharma and Brigadier Jasdeep Singh: All India Joint Armed Forces Institute, Volume 59, # 2, 2003.
66. Alexander B. Downes: Modern Insurgency and counter insurgency in comparative perspective: Civil Wars 9 no. 4, December 2007, pp. 313-23.
67. Chhattisgarh Home Minister Nanki Ram Kanwar told reporters on 15 February 2012 that police do not follow his order. He complained to them that on 12 February he had asked the SP of Korba to file a FIR against two police personnel of the Kotwali police station for molesting and attempting to rape a minor, daughter of Milon Das, resident of Dhanmarpara, in Korba district. However, the Korba SP dismissed these allegations and claimed he had not received any such order from the minister. The home minister told the media that there is a Supreme Court ruling stating that mere oral complaint by a girl victim is enough in such cases for filing a FIR. This is the same Chhattisgarh police that also eulogized as 'Chhattisgarh hero' a fugitive from justice and alleged rapist and killer Kartam Surya.

    Kartam Surya is a twenty-nine-year-old police constable who was one of the three 'informal' commanders of a band of approximately 100 SPOs dubbed as 'Koya Commandos'. After the Supreme Court declared as illegal the recruitment of SPOs, nearly all of them were absorbed in a special auxiliary force constituted by the Chhattisgarh government. However, Kartam Surya was accused of raping three tribal women, aged 19–23, at Sam Sehi village in the summer of 2006. On November 17, 2009, the sessions court issued a warrant against the accused including Kartam Surya. The prosecutor claimed that Kartam and others could not be tracked, although Kartam and other SPOs continued to engage in raid and search operations in Sukma district, living under police protection inside the police camp. Additional DG (Naxal) of police dismissed the warrant and accusation as being part of 'well conceived strategy of Naxals ...', the SP (Security) at Chhattisgarh police headquarters went so far as to say that

Kartam Surya 'was able to instill fear in ultras for his ruthlessness' and praised him for being the 'Chattisgarh hero'.

68. *Indian Express,* 17 July 2010.
69. *Times of India,* 10 January 2011.
70. *The Asian Age,* 2 June 2011.
71. Ibid.
72. *The Hindu,* 10 January 2011.
73. See *Days and Nights in the Heartland of Rebellion;* Penguin (India); New Delhi 2012; pp. 15-24.
74. PM's speeches, *http://pmindia.nic.in/.*
75. Strategy and Tactics of the Indian Revolution; released on 21 January 2007, p. 34.
76. Ibid; p. 36. The same document also says: 'Guerilla bases are transitory in nature and it is not a separate phase in itself. If we want to wage guerilla war powerfully, if we want to change the Guerilla zones into Liberated Areas, then the question of establishment of guerilla bases will have a special importance. These guerilla bases will constitute the focal points within the guerilla zones for the development of a strong party, a strong people's liberation army and a united front while, at the same time, creating favourable conditions for the establishment of liberated areas, expanding the political power in waves and quickening the tempo of the revolution. As the new political power in the guerilla bases goes on stabilizing, changes should be brought about in the production relations while intensifying the agrarian revolution. Land should be distributed on the basis of land to the tiller and cooperative movement among the people should be promoted for the development of agriculture. The embryonic form of the new democratic state should be consolidated. Therefore it should be understood that formation of the guerilla base means a significant advance in the process of building base area. This will create a strong impact on the people in the areas around the guerilla base and will inspire them to participate in the people's war more extensively.' p. 35.
77. *Interview of General Secretary of CPI (Maoist)* by Jan Myrdal and Gautam Navlakha in January 2010. Sanhati.com/articles/2138/.
78. Interview of Cherukuri Rajkumar, spokesperson of CPI (Maoist) with Siddartha Vardarajan. *The Hindu,* 14 April 2010.
79. *Indian Express,* 7 February 2013.

80. *Undated document but probably from after the Party congress in 2007.* It says:

> a) In some areas, the lands occupied from landlords in the past are lying fallow due to government repression; when the landlords try to sell these lands, the rich peasants and middle peasants are purchasing them. On such occasions, instead of bringing pressure through the agricultural labourers and poor peasants, who occupied those lands, on those who purchased the lands and stopping the sales, the squads themselves have been thrashing the rich and middle peasants who purchased the lands.
>
> b) In the struggle for the eradication of bad habits like liquor consumption, educating the people with a long term view is lacking; in the struggle to obstruct the manufacture of arrack, instead of rallying the people, especially the women, prominence is being given to squad actions only. Physical punishments are being imposed disregarding class basis.
>
> c) When problems arise in man-woman relations, especially in matters relating to marriage, judgments are being given without taking into view, the social problems women face.
>
> d) In various kinds of people's 'Panchayats' instead of listening to the versions of both sides apart from gathering the needed information from others in the villages also, one sided judgments are being delivered, under the effect of sectarianism.
>
> e) When some among the people commit mistakes, when they oppose our mass organisations, or when they are suspected to be working as informers, punishments much beyond their wrongs are being imposed.

81. This document refers to corrupting influence of contractors and middle men on party cadres. 'In recent years, large scale relief and reform programmes launched by the government have created a huge battery of contractors and middle-men in the rural area. They are the social basis of various groups of ruling class parties. Locally, they maintain links with organizers (comrades at zone and even higher levels), appease them, assure block officials and

engineers that they can 'manage' the 'new government' and get hold of contracts. During polls, these are the elements who wean away people to polling stations. *That relation with such type of contractors have been maintained by party organizers is a matter of concern.* Some of our comrades use such contractors not only for various work, but also the most secret work of the Party, and they also share their joys and sorrows. The tiffs between contractors over this or that contract has become a cause for contradiction between our cadres. Among cadres ill-feeling arise as they take sides between the contractors; different contractors even take recommendation letters of their "protector" party comrades to Block development Officials and engineers in order to win in the competition for contracts. For eg in Chatra, the so called contradiction between Yadavs and Ganjhus is not a contradiction between toiling masses of these two castes, but between contractors and middle-men of these castes.'

82. Clausewitz, On War http://www.marxists.org/reference/archive/clausewitz/works/on-war/index.htm
83. *In the Wake of Naxalbari*: Sumanta Bannerjee; Shishu Sahitya Samsad, Kolkata; p.129.
84. Interview of Kishenji, who headed the Eastern Regional Bureau of the CPI (Maoist). *Frontline*, 26 October-6 November, 2009. The Eastern Regional Bureau of the CPI (Maoists) was, reportedly, criticized by the Central Committee of the party for 'un-necessary killings'. (*Indian Express*, 14 November 2011).
85. Communist Party of India (Marxist) Draft Political Resolution for the 20[th] Party Congress.
86. Strategy and Tactics; ibid; p. 112.
87. Interview of Kishenji by Tusha Mittal; *Tehelka* Magazine, 13 November 2007. See also *Times of India* (Kolkata edition), 10 October 2002.
88. *Times of India*, 27 April 2009.
89. Ibid.
90. Letter of CPI (Maoist) to Santosh Rana and reply from the CPI (ML); 29 October 2009. http://en.atik-online.net/2009/10/29letter-of-thecpimaoists-to-santoshrana.
91. Strategy and Tactics; ibid., p. 122.
92. See Navlakha, Gautam (2010). Ibid., pp. 105–13.
93. *Frontline*, 26 October–6 November, 2009.

94. A Maoist leader in Orissa, Sabyasachi Panda, who broke away from the party, referring to similar such killings had admitted that cadres have been guilty of 'mistakes' and said that if 'somebody earns huge property we should not kill him. We should seize the property from him and distribute it among the destitute'. Also '[b]efore killing a political activist, we should expose him before the people'. But he was candid enough to agree that the party 'does not have the strength to give these cadres proper perspective about the revolution . . . An organization evolves from process of internal debate over several contentious issues. We will certainly rectify our mistakes. Cadres will be motivated to work in close coordination with people at the grass-root level'. *The Hindu*, 11 February 2012. The irony is that it was under his call that the assassination of Vishwa Hindu Parishad leader in Kandamahal took place and his forces were ill-prepared to meet the onslaught. So his criticism has to be tempered by his attempt to appear more responsible than the rest of the Party.
95. Bikash to the press on 15 June 2009.
96. See for details *Days and Nights in the Heartland of Rebellion*; Gautam Navlakha; Penguin (India) 2012.
97. Lenin; 'The Principles of Socialism and the War of 1914-15', 1915 http://www.marxists.org/archive/lenin/works/1915/s+w/ch01.htm
98. Interview of Cherukuri Rajkumar, spokesperson of CPI (Maoist) with Siddartha Vardarajan. *The Hindu*, 14 April 2010.
99. Schmitt. Ibid., p. 10.
100. *Times of India*, 3 February 2013.
101. *Times of India*, 30 January 2013.
102. The Geneva Conventions of 1949: origins and current significance; address by Philip Spoerri, Director of International Law, ICRC on 12 August 2009 on the occasion of the sixtieth anniversary of the Geneva Conventions.
103. Schmitt, Ibid; pp. 41-42.
104. Ibid. p. 65.
105. D'Mello, Bernard (2011) 'Insurgent Comrades: Maoist Learnings-by doing in India, 1967-2010' (unpublished). The Article 59 of the CPI (Maoist) Party Constitution says, 'The party fractions shall be formed in the executive committees of mass organizations. Party fractions will guide the executive committees of the mass organizations adopting suitable method in accordance with the

correct concrete situation. Fraction will function secretly. The opinions of party committee/member guiding the fraction shall be considered as final opinion. If fraction committee members have any difference of opinion, they will send their opinions in writing to the concerned party committee/higher committee. The concerned party committees shall guide fraction committees of different mass organizations at their own level.' The ambiguity of the above has actually seen that many cadres read it to justify commandism.

106. Deutscher, Issac (1964), Maoism: Its Origins, Background and Outlook; Socialist Register, 1964; pp. 30–32.
107. Schmitt, ibid; p. 64.
108. http://www.marxists.org/archive/lenin/works/1915/s+w/ch01.htm#v21fl70h-299

## Bibliography

1. D'Mello, Bernard (2011): 'Insurgent Comrades: Maoist Learning-by doing in India, 1967-2010' (unpublished).
2. Deutscher, Issac (1964): *Maoism: Its Origins, Background and Outlook*; Socialist Register, 1964.
3. Engels, Frederik: *Introduction to Class Struggles in France: 1848-1850*; Karl Marx; SW Vol I, Progress Publishers, Moscow 1973.
4. Galle, W.B. (1975): *Philosophers of War: Kant, Clausewitz, Marx, Engels and Tolstoy*, Cambridge University Press.
5. Guevara, Che (2012): *Guerilla Warfare*; Authorised edition with correction by the author; Leftword, Delhi, 2008.
6. Kaldor, Mary (2012): *New and Old Wars: Organised Violence in a Global Era*; Polity Press, Cambridge (UK) 2012.
7. Keegan, John (1994): *History of Warfare*; Vintage Books, New York 1994.
8. Kipnis, Andrew (2003): *The Anthropology of Power and Maoism*; American Anthropologist; 105 (2), 2003; pp. 278–88.
9. Lenin, VI (1906): *Guerilla Warfare*: Volume 11 of Collected Works, Progress Publications; Moscow.
10. Lenin, VI (1908): *Bellicose Militarism and the Anti-Militarist Tactics of Social Democrats*: Volume 15; CW, Moscow.
11. Lenin, VI (1915): *The Principles of Socialism and the War of 1914–15*; http://www.marxists.org/archive/lenin/works/1915/S+W/.
12. Lenin, VI: *The Military Programme of Proletarian Revolution*; http://www.marxists.org/archive/lenin/works/1916/miliprog/
13. Lew, Richard (1975): *Maoism and the Chinese Revolution*; Socialist Register, 1975.
14. Mao, ze Dong (1937): On Guerilla Warfare, http://www.marxists.org/reference/archive/mao/selected works/volume 2
15. Mao, ze Dong (1938): *Problems of War and Strategy*: http://www.marxists.org/reference/archive/mao/selected-works/volume-2/mswv2_12.htm
16. Mao, ze Dong, (1938): *On Protracted War*; http://www.marxists.org/refernce/archive/mao/selected-works/volume

17. Myrdal, Jan and Navlakha, Gautam (2010): Interview with General Secretary of CPI (Maoist), Ganapathy; January 2010; http://sanhati.com/articles/2138/
18. Navlakha, Gautam (2010): *Days and Nights in the Heartland of Rebellion*; Penguin (India) 2012.
19. Roy, Biswajeet (editor) (2012); *War and Peace in Junglemahal: People, State and the Maoists;* Setu Prakashani, Kolkata.
20. Schmitt, Carl (2004) *The Theory of the Partisan: A Commentary/Remark on the Concept of the Political;* Translated by A.C. Goodson; Michigan State University Press.
21. Singh, Randhir (2008): *Socialism & Indian Politics: A View from the Left*; Aakar Books, Delhi 2008.

## CPI (Maoist) Documents Consulted

1. *Strategy and Tactics of the Indian Revolution*; released on 21 January 2007.
2. *New Circular on Rectification* (undated but issued post 2007 Ninth Congress of the Party).
3. *Bihar–Jharkhand Special Area Committee on 'Rectification': People's War* (October 2004–September 2005).
4. *Policy Program of Revolutionary People's Committee*; released by the CC of CPI (Maoist) on 12 December 2007.

*Annexure*

# Principled versus Piecemeal Approach: AFSPA, Troops Pullout or Ending War against Our People

In order to understand the significance of the Armed Forces Special Powers Act and our response, we must understand the role of the Armed Forces of the Union in wars of suppression. It is my contention that our opposition to AFSPA is not *only* because it protects the Armed Forces of the Union (which is how the Indian Constitution defines the Army, Navy, Air Force and the Central Paramilitary Forces) but *also* because we, in the Civil Liberties and Democratic Rights groups, oppose the policy of military suppression of our own people in the first place (at least, formally considered 'our own'), because it is this that necessitates protection for military forces deployed to carry out the dirty task of brutally restoring the State's authority, in turn creating the source legitimacy for counter-violence.

Out of 626 districts in India, no less than 136 districts, with a population in excess of 150 million, witness this policy of military suppression. Of these 136 districts, 101 have been notified as 'disturbed areas' where AFSPA and state-level Disturbed Areas Act, either separately or concurrently, operate. In thirty-five of the so-called joint forces operations against 'Left Wing Extremists', neither of these Acts are invoked and yet the war continues. (Of course, there could be in places like Chhattisgarh, Bihar, Orissa, Jharkhand, Andhra Pradesh, Maharashtra, West Bengal, some other state-level Act in operation indemnifying the forces.) However, for all practical purposes, the ground reality is no different in these thirty-five districts spread over nine states and the 101 districts where AFSPA is notified.

The second thing to note is that the Central government has set aside Rs 40,000 crore for 'internal security' (which falls under the Ministry of Home Affairs), i.e., for wars in these districts where nearly 80 per cent of the Central Paramilitary Forces (whose strength is 9,00,000 plus 145 battalions of India Reserve Batallion, or 1,50,000 personnel) and half of the Indian Army (3,37,000 in J&K, and 2,80,000 in entire NE) is engaged in counter-insurgency. Were we to add to this Rs 40,000 crore allocated towards 'internal security' with what the Ministry of Defence spends on 'internal security' (merely taking the wages, allowances and pension of this force into account), which comes to approximately Rs 29,000 crore, the Indian government is spending a staggering sum of Rs 69,000 crore annually to pay for these wars. This amount could suffice to pay for a universal Food Security Act in India. Significantly, the Union Finance Ministry has cited paucity of funds to pay for a universal Food Security Act.

There is another dimension to this which needs to be considered. In an interview to *Tehelka* (5 June 2010), Union Home Secretary G.K. Pillai said that 'Manipur has the highest police to population ratio in the country'. And yet, Manipur is raising another four battalions of Manipur Commandos! Of course, he did not spell out what the ratio was. J&K, according to Chief Minister Omar Abdullah, has anywhere between 5 to 7 lakh troops (army, CPMFs, State

Armed Police, etc.) for a population that is said to be 1.1 crore. This means a ratio of one armed soldier for twenty persons. Of course, the ratio changes even more if we consider the actual concentration of troops in the Kashmir valley and those districts of Jammu which have sizable Muslim population. It could be approximately one armed soldier for fifteen persons or even less. Thus, the ratio could be a lot worse than what was cited by the Home Secretary in the case of Manipur. Such a heavy concentration of forces deployed in a manner that monitors and controls the public and private lives of people creates impediments in the way of normal activities of people and causes a heavy loss of scarce human and material resources whose actual cost is yet to be calculated.

To this one ought to add another dimension. As is evident from the case in J&K, there is pressure on the J&K government to recruit and train quickly a force which can replace the Central forces. Thus, accretion in the strength of the armed police gets compounded because apart from bloated CPMFs, we now have bloated state-level armed police formations. And like the Central forces being protected by AFSPA, these State forces have their own state-level protective safeguards against prosecution for any act committed in course of 'active service'.

In other words, these conflicts become the occasion for stupendous augmentation of personnel in the existing armed formations (in 2007–08, Shivraj Patil, the then Union Home Minister, spoke of raising 206 battalions of CPMFs over the next five years) and/or through creation of new forces of either armed police battalions or entities such as the Rashtriya Rifles, which was raised for fighting insurgency in J&K in 1993–94. It is also less known that the armed police is trained along the lines of the infantry formations of the Indian Army. Keep in mind also the fact since 1947, not a year has passed when the Indian State has not been engaged in waging an internal war (call it by any name, war/armed conflict/military suppression) against our own people in some part of the country or the other. It can also be established empirically that almost all movements that picked up guns did so only after non-violent struggles were run aground by the Indian State one way or the other, or dismissed out of hand. In all these cases of internal wars, military (the army and CPMFs in particular) is deployed for a prolonged period with enhanced powers to act on their own, i.e., minus civilian supervision. This is unlike their short-term usage during instances like riots where they operate under the orders of the magistrate and are protected under S 45 (Protection of Members of the Armed Forces from Arrest) of the CrPC. This is the background in which the campaign to repeal AFSPA is located.

When AFSPA was passed in 1958, after a truncated debate in the Parliament, the then Union Home Minister G.B. Pant had assured the members of Parliament that the Act was temporary and only confined to fighting the 'Naga hostiles'. What was temporary became a permanent feature and can now be imposed anywhere in the Indian Union. The Parliament also never saw it fit to debate/review this Act since its enactment. Prior to the UPA government instituting this review process, the Indian Supreme Court had examined this Act. The judicial process had resulted in the Supreme Court in 1997 upholding the legal validity of AFSPA, asserting that Parliament had the powers to enact such an Act. The review of the Act undertaken by the Justice Jeevan Reddy Committee as per its Terms of Reference was not mandated to recommend its repeal. However, having decided to ask for its repeal, it went on to suggest that provisions of the Act could be incorporated into the

Unlawful Activities Prevention Act 2004. Thus, both the Supreme Court in its 1997 judgment as well as the Justice Reddy Committee in its report have upheld the need to empower the Armed Forces of the Union when they are deployed for prolonged period in an area declared to be 'Disturbed'. The other drawback of the Reddy Committee was that the review and public hearings that followed were confined to the North-East, particularly Manipur and Assam. The conspicuous absence of J&K from its purview was most unfortunate.

It needs to be reiterated that the AFSPA has been introduced *not* to curb armed militancy but it is meant to control the civilian population from extending support to secessionist activities. Thus the Act antagonizes more and more people and swells the ranks of militants, contrary to the official pretence that they are fighting only the armed groups.

This is clear from the ground reality of J&K with a huge deployment exceeding six lakh troops (which comprise the army, CPMFs, the State Armed Police, etc.). Bunkers, checkpoints, road blocks are manned by CRPF/BSF in towns while Rashtriya Rifles (the Indian Army's sixty-six-battalion-strong counter-insurgency force) maintains vigil in the rural areas. Virtually every neighbourhood in the urban area boasts a camp of security forces and between every forty-five villages, there is a camp of the RR. Srinagar town alone has 400 bunkers, thus the recent removal of sixteen of them is inconsequential. This level of deployment continues at a time when it is officially claimed that the number of militants is no more than 600 and that no more than 250 of them remain in the Kashmir valley. Such a heavy security presence means that the movement of people on roads and bazar is regulated, with them being frequently asked to show their IDs, and their bags being searched. It is a known fact that anyone in a

'Disturbed' area found without an ID can suffer anything from having to bribe his way to freedom to becoming a victim of enforced disappearance.

Again the very deployment of the security forces necessitates occupation of land and buildings. On 24 August 2009, the state government had informed the J&K Assembly that out of 1,054,721 kanals (or 1,31,840 acres), spread over eighty-two tehsils of J&K, occupied by the Indian security forces, only 1,99,314 kanals (24,914.25 acres) were under the lease licence and acquisitions made under the provision of the Land Acquisition Act. Thus, nearly 80 per cent of the land was under illegal occupation. As a result, when the Union Ministry of Defence announced with much fanfare that they were increasing the rental for the lands and buildings that they are occupying, they obviously meant that they would be paying higher rent for the land leased since there is no question of paying rent for land illegally occupied.

They also occupy more than 1572 buildings, which includes ninety-eight schools. This impacts normal life and economic activities. However, all this is a quintessential aspect of counter-insurgency policy, which is meant to break the link between the armed groups and the people through recourse to force or threat of use of force.

In other words, while atrocities may come down if the legal cover indemnifying the security forces is withdrawn, it would be naïve to believe that the atrocities will *cease* if this cover is withdrawn. Because atrocities are inherent in the very nature of counter-insurgency, whose main purpose is to coerce a people into submission.

The findings of civil liberties groups, as well as of official inquiries undertaken from time to time, show that once AFSPA comes into operation, the civil administration begins to play second fiddle. Instead of 'coming to the aid of civil administration', the forces virtually replace them. Thus, the overlap between law and order which pertains to the civilian domain and internal security, which is the raison d'être of AFSPA, is difficult to keep apart. In real life, the lines get blurred to the point that even traffic management invites the overbearing presence of the AFU. Lately, AFU have been entrusted with running of schools, health centres, road building and construction and management of micro-hydel projects (as in J&K). More and more matters that were considered part of the civil administration are becoming part of AFU activity, all in the name of WHAM (Winning Hearts and Minds), or Operation Sadbhavna.

We have in recent times also witnessed the heads of coordination centres, invariably corps commanders belonging to the army, intervening in the public domain with their own assessment of the situation. The most reprehensible was the statement of the GOC-in-C of the Northern Command who characterized non-violent protests in Kashmir as being 'agitational terrorism'. It amounts to declaring all protestors as 'terrorists' and thus made them legitimate targets of the firepower of the security forces. Between 11 June 2010 and 15 October 2010, there have been 110 civilian deaths (all victims of bullets, tear gas shells, torture), 1500 cases of firearm/tear gas shell/pellet injuries, 500 cases of severe beatings and thirty-eight instances of blindness caused by bullet/pellet/marbles used as projectile in the slingshots used by the CRPF. Despite these killings and serious injuries, just a single FIR has been filed in a single case against the CRPF for unauthorized killing of a youth, but no one has been arrested. In other words, civilian protestors are easy pickings. The problem gets compounded because promotion and reward provide material incentive for the security personnel to carry out extra-judicial killings.

Often, the officers of the security forces adopt a position which is at odds with that of the political authority. A recent such case was witnessed in Assam where both the Corps Commander as well as the Governor (usually a retired general) came out opposing a political initiative to begin dialogue with ULFA. Such a situation is a direct fallout of employing security forces over a long duration in internal situations, which creates a kind of vested interest and where they come to enjoy untrammeled power.

Arguably, as the situation worsens with recourse to military suppression, it throws up its own compulsions where some militant or renegade groups begin to browbeat the civilians. There are times when inimical neighbours exploit this situation to fan the fuels of militancy. I believe that such a situation can be dealt with most effectively only when there is a political process and the government appears sincere and serious in addressing the legitimate grievances, and takes recourse to democratic solutions. The solution would be different from respecting right to self-determination in Kashmir or Manipur or Naga areas, and pursuing the path of dialogue with the Maoists to address structural reforms. To believe that problems get resolved when people are suppressed is contrary to ground reality. Developments in J&K are a reminder that despite the most horrendous twenty years of repression and the most extraordinary control that grips the lives of people in Kashmir, the demand for 'azadi' from India remains robust.

Now having gone through the debate over AFSPA for over three decades, our struggle saw the Supreme Court uphold the constitutional validity of the Act (in NPMHR vs Union of India, 1997) albeit suggesting some minimal safeguards in the shape of a half-yearly review of its working or defining strictly what the 'shortest possible time' is for handing over a person arrested by the Armed Forces of the Union to the police . The next round of our collective efforts saw the appointment of Justice Jeevan Reddy Committee (2004–05) which called for the repeal of AFSPA, because the title had come to acquire a pejorative meaning; therefore, he suggested that AFSPA's provisions should be incorporated into the Unlawful Activities Prevention Act. And now, even as the demand grows for repeal of AFSPA, to coincide with ten years of Irom Sharmila's fast-unto-death, there are efforts afoot to persuade us that we should become pragmatic/realistic and settle for dilution of some provisions or amendments to certain sections of AFSPA or for its step-by-step withdrawal from a state. Thus the struggle is not only confined to one part of a larger problem, i.e., AFSPA; it now gets further complicated (or weakened) with a call for being sensible and to settle for dilution/partial withdrawal.

While it is correct that the removal of AFSPA could mean withdrawal of the army – in particular from CI duties which forms part of its secondary role – since the army does not want to operate without indemnity against prosecution, it is futile to believe that in the face of near unanimity in the Parliament among the political parties, the powers enjoyed by the AFU in the 'Disturbed' areas will get curbed and we will get only dilution/partial withdrawal of AFSPA. It would *not* mean an end to military suppression/armed conflict per se. Because the armed constabularies of the state too are deployed, and looking at the experience of Manipur or J&K and the role of the state-level forces in the nine states where joint operations are going on against the Maoists, there is absolutely no reason to believe that they are any less brutal and dastardly. This is evident from the recent incidents in Manipur perpetrated by the Manipur commandos, or in J&K where large-scale war crimes have been committed by the Special Operations Group/Special Task Force of the J&K Police or the horrendous record of the forces of nine states where anti-Maoists operations are going on. Thus, for one, we might get rid of AFSPA and the army partially. And secondly, we will see them get replaced by state armed forces and state-level DAA. In other words, our major concern about ending the use of military suppression to resolve political problems will not be addressed. All in all, a piecemeal approach focuses on merely one aspect of the conflict.

The conventional wisdom is that this is better than nothing or that at least this can provide immediate relief for civilians in the conflict zone. While this appears attractive, it does not unfortunately resolve the predicament we face, which has become worse now that there is a near-unanimous consensus among all the parliamentary parties, from left to right, against the repeal of AFSPA, and there exists only a fractured support even for pulling out the army from the theatre of internal war/s.

If one has to settle for a piecemeal approach, why should we not replace the call for repeal of AFSPA with a call for withdrawal of the military forces? If we have to have a piecemeal approach, why not explore the possibility of achieving our objective by demanding the withdrawal of the army and the CPMFs from counter-insurgency operations? There are many retired and serving army officers who believe that the army's primary responsibility has been compromised and its discipline has been affected by making it focus more on its secondary role (of aiding civil administration in times of conflict or calamity). They also feel that while protection is essential if the army is called in and therefore AFSPA should remain, they favour withdrawal of the army from CI as being necessary.

Besides, calling for repeal of AFSPA has been made complex with most political parties (including the Left parties and Congress) in favour of pulling out the army. But they are not in favour of repeal of AFSPA or its revocation where the army has been deployed.

However, even this leaves much to be desired. Because, there is another section of armed forces that favours the army's induction in internal security affairs since power and pelf accompany such a role. They also happen to outnumber those who are against it. This view is not only the official position – indeed, the army is engaged in honing its CI skills as illustrated by its doctrine of sub-conventional warfare and doctrine of perception management (an important part of CI).. Something unstated is also the fact that 'disturbed areas' provide the army an occasion to shake off civilian control and garner resources. Thus, the call for pull-out of the army has been also countered by saying that Article 355 of the Constitution read together with 2(A) of the Union List, empowers the Central government to deploy Central forces in situations of internal security. And that whatever may have been the cause once, if there is rebellion it has to be put down, if need be by the army. So a fait accompli is offered to us.

Thus, it is abundantly clear that a piecemeal approach, either demanding the repeal of AFSPA or withdrawal of the army, are not without problems and do not adequately address the problem. I am reminded of what happened when POTA was revoked. We were told by many a progressive commentator to be happy at that half-victory since the clause of confession to police, while in their custody, was dropped. What these progressives failed to realize was that the rest of POTA got incorporated into the Unlawful Activities Prevention Act 1967 (which got further strengthened in 2004 and then again in 2008), and which by now has become even more lethal a threat than TADA or POTA.

Take another example. The Indian government offered a sop to people after the rape and murder of Manorama Devi by the Assam Rifles, in the shape of withdrawal of AFSPA from Imphal. The result was that instead of the Assam Rifles, now Manipur Commandos carry out the killing in Imphal (and elsewhere too) since they enjoy the protection provided by the state government. Thus, AFSPA may not be in operation in Imphal but conditions in Imphal are no different, and no better, than elsewhere in Manipur. The point being that very often, a half-measure ends up biting us and leaves us worse off than before.

Will this mean that non-state groups can continue fighting while the State demilitarizes? I doubt it. A 'no' to war against our own people robs even the non-state actors of their source of legitimacy. If the state does not wage war, i.e., there is no prolonged deployment and empowerment of military forces against our own people, why would people or any political group take up arms? If there is a possibility of non-violently resolving matters, including possibilities of transforming State and society, why would anyone take to armed resistance? There is no natural propensity of people to opt for armed resistance. The prospects of people taking to arms is directly linked to the Indian State's propensity to use military suppression as the mother of all policies against popular movements demanding either the right of self-determination or radical transformation.

But are there not groups that possess weapons or believe in armed resistance? Mere possession of weapons does not mean declaration of war against the State. Also, opting for armed resistance is never an automatic choice; rather it is a proposition that is contested and debated within the revolutionary parties and liberation groups prior to the decision being taken. In an interview given to *The Hindu* (14 April 2010), Cherukuri Rajkumar, aka., Azad, had reminded that it was the 'imposition of the ban (against the CPI [ML] [PW]) that had led the party and the mass organizations to take up arms in the first place . . . What shook the rulers at that time (in 1978) and compelled them to declare Jagtyala and Sircila talukas in Karimnagar district of north Telengana as disturbed areas in 1978 was not the armed struggle of the Maoists (which had suffered a complete setback . . . by 1972) but the powerful (movement against) the anti-feudal order in the countryside . . .' Were the State not to wage war against its people, the chances of the debate veering towards armed resistance gets reduced.

It is also worth remembering that there are, according to the International Action Network on Small Arms, an estimated forty million private weapons in India. It does not require rocket science to believe that these tens of millions of weapons are mostly in the possession of people in Indian society who wield power and are privileged. This reality, and an India, which for all its verbosity about non-violence, is one of the most heavily armed States both in terms of accumulation of destructive power of its arsenal as well as the size of its military force which gets force multiplied by draconian laws, enables the ruling classes to remain lukewarm/indifferent to the most inhuman working and living conditions for the majority of our people. Therefore, I believe we should be pitching for something that helps us focus on the fundamental concern and not its symptom (militancy being in essence a manifestation against oppression) to enable us to argue for a peaceful and democratic way out. Thus, we should be opposing the war-making proclivities of the government.

In other words, ten years of Irom Sharmila's heroic fast and more than four decades of struggle against AFSPA should convince us that the time has come for us to demand an end to war against our own people as the principled and realistic stance. Once we accept the legitimacy of wars against our own people, we enable the State to argue for AFSPA, DAA, etc. Of course, those who believe that AFSPA alone should be repealed but wars against our own people should carry on will oppose this because they believe that no State can allow any non-State group to overthrow it. But they must have the courage of their conviction to come out and say so rather than hide behind the façade of being 'pacifist', while intellectually supporting the policy of military suppression and the bloodletting that ensues. But those of us who argue that the State must give up prosecuting wars against our own people must seriously consider a course correction lest we are led to the 'desolation row' through a piecemeal effort.